# your RE
## PUPIL BOOK

**Series Editor:**
Jon Mayled

**Authors:**
Katie Clemmey
Janet Dyson
Tanya Hill
Jon Mayled
Peter Smith

www.pearsonschoolsandfecolleges.co.uk
✓ Free online support
✓ Useful weblinks
✓ 24 hour online ordering

0845 630 33 33

Heinemann
Part of Pearson

Heinemann is an imprint of Pearson Education Limited, a company incorporated in England and Wales, having its registered office at Edinburgh Gate, Harlow, Essex CM20 2JE. Registered company number: 872828

www.pearsonschoolsandfecolleges.co.uk

Heinemann is a registered trademark of Pearson Education Limited.

Text © Pearson Education Limited 2011

First published 2011

15 14 13 12
10 9 8 7 6 5 4 3 2

**British Library Cataloguing in Publication Data**
A catalogue record for this book is available from the British Library.

ISBN 978 0 435 04668 2

Designed by Pearson Education Limited

Typeset by Christopher Howson (look2design)

Original illustrations © Pearson Education Limited 2011

Illustrated by Pearson Education Limited and MN Digital Graphics

Cover design by Pearson Education Limited

Picture research by Ginny Stroud-Lewis

Printed in Malaysia, CTP-PJB

**Websites**
There are links to relevant websites in this product. In order to ensure that the links are up to date, that the links work, and that the sites are not inadvertently linked to sites that could be considered offensive, we have made the links available on the Heinemann website at www.pearsonschoolsandfecolleges.co.uk/hotlinks. When you access the site, the express code is 6682.

The authors and publisher would like to express their thanks to the following individuals, organisations and schools for their help with developing and testing the material in this book. Any errors or misrepresentations are the responsibility of the publisher.

Paul Cullen, Head of RE, St Bernard's Catholic School, High Wycombe

Patrick Garton, Head of the RS/PSHCE Faculty, Cherwell School, Oxford

Arabella Northey, Head of RE, Blessed Hugh Faringdon Catholic School, Reading

Emily Pearson, Head of RE, Kennet School, Thatcham

Luke Salkeid, Head of RE, St Edmund Campion School, Birmingham

Kristina Shakeshaft, Subject Leader RE, The Arthur Terry School, Sutton Coldfield

Michelle Smith, Head of RE, John Willmott School, Sutton Coldfield

Steven Spriggs, Head of RE, Coventry Bluecoat CE School

**Faith readers**
**Bahá'í Faith** – Stephen Vickers, Chair, The UK Bahá'í Religious Education Agency

**Buddhism** – Desmond Biddulph, Chair, The Buddhist Society London

**Christianity** – Dick Powell, Project Associate, The Culham Institute, Oxford; Father Tim Gardner OP, RE Adviser, The Catholic Education Service for England and Wales; Sarah Lane Cawte, Education Officer, Free Church Education Unit

**Hinduism** – Rasamandala Das, Mandala Education

**Humanism** – Andrew Copson, Chief Executive, British Humanist Association

**Islam** – Ghulam Sarwar, Chair, Muslim Educational Trust; Imran Mogra, Birmingham City University

**Jainism** – Mehool H. Sanghrajka, Director of Education, Institute of Jainology Limited

**Judaism** – Hannah Ashleigh, Education Policy and Projects Manager, Board of Deputies of British Jews; Rabbi Sybil Sheridan, Wimbledon & District Synagogue

**Sikhism** – Richard Gray

**Zoroastrianism** – John Hinnells, Emeritus Professor in the Comparative Study of Religions and Honorary Research Professorial Fellow at the School of Oriental and African Studies, London University, Senior Member of Robinson College, Cambridge and Life Fellow of Clare Hall, Cambridge

# Contents

# Introduction

## Why study Religious Education?

Religious Education is an important subject because every area of life is touched by issues to do with religion and belief. Studying Religious Education can enable you to develop the skills, insights and understanding you need in today's world.

As young people who are growing up in a diverse society, studying religion will help you to understand and relate to people whose beliefs, values and viewpoints may be different from your own. It will enable you to deal with issues that arise, not only in school but also in the community. The study of religion will also help you to make connections with a range of other subject areas, such as music, literature, art, politics, economics and social sciences.

## Your RE

*Your RE* explores what people of different faiths understand about God, authority, worship, beliefs, values and truth. It provides opportunities to consider why people believe in God and how their beliefs can influence many aspects of their lives. It also looks at why members of a particular religion may believe different things. As you study the course you will have the chance to think, talk, discuss, question and challenge, as you reflect on and assess a wide range of questions. You will learn how to use your knowledge and understanding as well as your reasoning skills.

The course will allow you to study Christianity in depth and learn about nine other religions and belief systems: Bahá'í Faith, Buddhism, Hinduism, Humanism, Islam, Jainism, Judaism, Sikhism and Zoroastrianism.

The course is presented through a printed Pupil Book and an interactive CD-ROM.

## Pupil Book

The Pupil Book has been written especially for pupils aged 11–14 who are studying Religious Education.

The book contains eight chapters, each focusing on a different topic.

Chapter 1: What is authority?

Chapter 2: Spirituality

Chapter 3: Beliefs about God and the meaning of life

Chapter 4: Good and bad

Chapter 5: Rights and responsibilities

Chapter 6: Religion in the world

Chapter 7: Religion and science

Chapter 8: Can we all get on?

Each chapter starts with a two-page overview of the topic and this is followed by a number of sections which concentrate on different aspects.

Each section is made up of:

- Lesson 1, which considers the topic from a Christian point of view, with lesson objectives, key words and questions to help consolidate learning

- Lesson 2, which provides an insight into the views of nine other religions and belief systems, supported by questions to test understanding and apply what has been learned.

The last page of each chapter contains Your Assessment, which is an activity to bring together everything you have learned from the chapter.

At the end of the book, the key words are brought together in a Glossary, which you can refer to throughout the course.

## ActiveTeach CD-ROM

The CD-ROM provides:

- text pages and PowerPoint® slides containing extra information on all the religions introduced in the Pupil Book

- further resources to add interest and extend learning:
  - interactive activities to test knowledge
  - audio clips and transcripts to introduce extracts from sacred texts and other written and spoken sources of information
  - video clips to illustrate the information on the religions.

## Further resources

For more information on all of the religions and belief systems introduced and discussed in *Your RE*, we recommend that you visit the REonline website: http://www.reonline.org.uk.

REonline is a collaborative project, funded by the Association of Church College Trusts (ACCT) and managed on its behalf by the Culham Institute. It aims to provide information for all those working and interested in Religious Education.

**RE**online

## Note about conventions used

### Dates

The abbreviations BCE (Before the Common Era) and CE (Common Era) are used throughout to indicate dates before and after the birth of Jesus, which is traditionally taken to be Year 1. The abbreviations replace BC (Before Christ) and AD (*Anno Domini*, 'In the year of Our Lord'), which have a specifically Christian usage.

### Languages

There are many words in the book which come from languages other than English and which do not use the Roman alphabet. These include Apabhramsha, Arabic, Aramaic, Avestan, Dari, Greek, Hebrew, Pali, Persian, Prakrit, Punjabi and Sanskrit.

For Buddhism, Christianity, Hinduism, Islam, Judaism and Sikhism the transliterated spellings all follow the preferred forms found in the QCA Glossary of Religious Terms. In Buddhism, the Pali term is followed by the Sanskrit wherever appropriate.

### Religions

### Islam

ﷺ This symbol is composed of the words '*Salla-illahu alaihi wa sallam*' in Arabic - 'Peace and blessings of Allah upon him'. They are used by Muslims every time the name of the Prophet Muhammad is mentioned. Sometimes the words 'Peace be upon him' or the abbreviation 'Pbuh' are used.

### Judaism

The name of G-d which was given to the Jewish religious leader and prophet Moses is so sacred that it was only known to the High Priest of the Jerusalem Temple who spoke it once a year, alone in the Holy of Holies. Many Jews will not write the word which is a translation of this name and instead use the form G-d.

Throughout this book the latter two conventions have been followed, out of respect.

## Contributors

The people who have planned and contributed to Your RE include teachers, advisers, inspectors, teacher trainers and examiners, all of whom have specialist knowledge of Religious Education. All of us are fascinated by the subject and believe that pupils need good resources to use in the classroom. We also want to help make the subject lively, interactive and relevant to today's world, to encourage you to talk to each other and work together, to challenge you to think in depth in order to reach a high level of critical thinking, and to help you to organise your thoughts in writing in a persuasive and structured way.

We hope you enjoy studying *Your RE*.

Jon Mayled
Series Editor
January 2011

# Acknowledgements

The authors and publisher would like to thank the following individuals and organisations for permission to reproduce material in this book.

Photos

Pages 2–3 RTimages/Shutterstock; Alamy/Ben Molyneux People; AVAVA/Shutterstock; Monika Wisniewska/Shutterstock; Tim Graham/Alamy; Getty Images; page 5 Getty Images/AFP; page 9 Alamy/imagebroker; page 13 Alamy/MarioPonta; page 17 Dr_Flash/Shutterstock; page 21 Lane V. Erickson/Shutterstock; pages 24–5 BestPhoto1/Shutterstock; page 27 Roman Sigaev/Shutterstock; page 31 Tiut Lucian/Shutterstock; page 35 Elizabeth Barakah Hodges/Getty Images; page 51 Corbis/MAXPPP/JOSE NAVARRO/ep; page 55 Mike VON BERGEN/Shutterstock; page 63 VanHart/Shutterstock; pages 66–7 P.Jurik/Shutterstock; page 69 nld/Shutterstock; page 77 Peter Barritt/Alamy; page 81 Zvonimir Atletic/Shutterstock; page 85 Alamy/Michele Falzone; page 89 SuperStock/Getty Images; page 93 Kitch Bain/Shutterstock; page 97 Bruce Rolff/Shutterstock; pages 108–9 Dm73/Shutterstock; page 111 Mike Abrahams/Alamy; page 115 Getty Images/AFP; page 119 Michael Jenner/Alamy; page 123 Getty Images/AFP; page 127 Duncan Walker/iStockphoto; pages 134–5 Boguslaw Mazur/Shutterstock; page 136 oliveromg/Shutterstock; page 137 Corbis/Jose Nicolas/Sygma; page 138 Getty Images; page 138 Mark Richardson/Alamy; page 145 Corbis/Bernard Annebicque/Sygma; page 149 Alamy/Nathan King; page 153 Getty Images/The Image Bank/Sharon Montrose; page 157 Photolibrary; page 160 Alamy/Robert W. Ginn; page 165 Alamy/Chris Deeney; pages 168–9 Shutterstock/Vladimir Ivanovski; page 171 Alamy/© Picture Contact BV; page 174 Shutterstock/Picsfive; Corbis/Massimo Borchi; page 178 Alamy/INTERFOTO; page 183 Alamy/Ed Maynard; page 187 Alamy/PhotoAlto; page 191 Getty Images; page 195 Igor Shikov/Shutterstock; pages 198–9 Alamy/VIEW Pictures Ltd; page 201 Alamy/ICP; page 205 VladKol/Shutterstock; page 209 Jiri Vaclavek/Shutterstock; page 213 Alamy/North Wind Picture Archives; page 217 Alamy/Keystone Pictures USA; page 220 StockLite/Shutterstock; page 225 Corbis/Catherine Ivill/AMA; pages 228–9 Alamy/moodboard; page 231 Corbis/Jose Luis Pelaez, Inc./Blend Images; page 239 Alamy/The Art Gallery Collection; page 243 Rex Features.

Text

Scripture taken from the Holy Bible, New International Version®. Copyright © 1973, 1978, 1984 International Bible Society. Used by permission of Zondervan. All rights reserved.

Page 12 Words spoken during ordination © Archbishops Council. Used by permission.

Page 235 Quotation used by permission of The Inter Faith Network for the UK (www.interfaith.org.uk).

Every effort has been made to contact copyright holders of material reproduced in this book. Any omissions will be rectified in subsequent printings if notice is given to the publisher.

## The bigger picture

The pictures on this page should give you a lot of clues about what authority means, because they show people who have authority over others. A person who has authority over others – as a result of their job, their position in life or special qualities they have – has the right to expect these other people to do as they ask. If people refuse the requests of someone in authority, they may get into trouble.

A good example of this is a teacher. Teachers have authority over pupils so that they can help them learn. If you challenge your teacher's authority over you, by not doing your homework, for example, you will probably get into trouble.

Religion can be seen in a similar way: followers of a religion are given guidance in the form of rules to help them to behave in the way their religious leaders who have authority over them would like them to. What makes religions different, however, is that:

- the main figure of authority is not a person but something or someone else, such as God

- they have special books such as the Bible, which followers believe are written sources of authority from leaders in the past, many of whom they believe were inspired by God.

## Learning about religion

1  Use the information and pictures below to write your own full explanation of what the word 'authority' means.

2  Make a list of people who have authority over you. For each one, explain why they have authority over you.

3  Why do you think some books are said to have authority?

### Your discussion

Why do you think religious people might accept that their religious leaders have authority over them?

# 1 Introduction

## What is authority?

### Your lesson objectives

**In this lesson you will:**

- evaluate the importance of people having authority
- consider the authority of religious leaders.

### Your key words

**authority**

the power or right to be a leader of others

**Bible**

a word used for the sacred writing of the Jews (Tenakh) and Christians (Old and New Testaments)

**denomination**

a branch of a religion

**Eucharist**

a service celebrating the sacrifice of the death and resurrection of Jesus Christ, using bread and wine. This is sometimes called Holy Communion (Protestant), Liturgy (Orthodox) or Mass (Roman Catholic)

**infallible**

not capable of being wrong

**moral**

concerned with the principles of right and wrong

**Pope**

the Bishop of Rome who is the leader of the Roman Catholic Church

**priest**

a person with the authority to perform religious ceremonies

**worship**

to show love, respect or devotion to someone or something

### No one has authority over me!

Imagine what life would be like if someone decided that no one should have **authority** over them. What would stop them from breaking into other people's houses and stealing their possessions? Or driving past a school at 150 miles per hour at the end of the school day? Rather than thinking that authority is stopping us from doing what we want to do, perhaps we should think of it as stopping others from doing things that may hurt us. This is why we have laws and people like police officers and judges who have the authority to enforce them.

### Authority in religions

Most religions have people who show their authority over believers, in a way that is intended to be positive and helpful.

Christianity is made up of different groups called **denominations**. These include Roman Catholic, Church of England, Baptist, Methodist, Orthodox and the Religious Society of Friends (Quakers) among others. The largest denomination in the UK is the Church of England, but worldwide there are more Roman Catholics than any other type of Christian.

One of the biggest differences between the Roman Catholic Church and other denominations involves different sources of authority. The leader of the Roman Catholic Church is the **Pope**. The Pope has a special role as the successor of St Peter. When he speaks in this role what he says is believed to be **infallible** – that is, it must be true. Another source of authority in the Roman Catholic Church is the Magisterium, the teaching authority formed by the Pope and the bishops.

Pope Benedict XVI speaking to crowds in St Peter's Square, Vatican City.

The Protestant Churches do not agree that the authority of the Pope comes directly from God. Although some Protestants agree with some of the Pope's ideas, they may also think that some of what he says is wrong. They prefer to look in the **Bible** for answers to religious or **moral** questions. Protestant Churches do have people with the authority to lead their followers, but they are not thought to have the complete authority of God. Many Protestant Churches refer to the 'priesthood of all believers', the idea that all Christians should preach and teach the faith.

Both Roman Catholics and Protestants also have local people with authority. **Worship** in individual churches is led by a **priest** (also known as a vicar or minister). Priests have authority given to them by the Church, which allows them to lead worship, forgive sins and celebrate the **Eucharist**.

## Learning about religion

1 Imagine that you are in the crowd shown in the picture. Write down everything you would see that suggests power and authority.

2 Explain what Roman Catholics believe about the Pope.

3 Make a list of things a priest does.

# 1 Introduction

## What is authority?

### Bahá'í
Bahá'ís believe in the authority of the teachings of Bahá'u'lláh, which contain the laws and rules of their faith so that they can live according to God's will.

### Hinduism
Hindus believe that all authority comes from God. They also place authority in sacred texts such as the Vedas and Upanishads, in the *guru* (spiritual teacher) and in *sadhus* (holy people).

### Islam
Muslims believe that all authority comes from the one God, Allah. They believe that they can find Allah's will in the Qur'an, which contains God's words.

### Judaism
Jews believe that all authority comes from G-d. They believe that they can find his will through their scriptures, the Oral and Written Torah.

### Sikhism
Sikh beliefs about God's authority are found in the lives and teachings of the human *gurus* and in the Sikh sacred text, the Guru Granth Sahib Ji.

### Buddhism
Buddhism is a complete way of life that follows the teachings (*Dhamma/ Dharma*) of the best-known Buddha – Siddatha Gotama/Siddartha Gautama. These teachings help Buddhists to follow a lifestyle that leads to happiness and reduces suffering.

### Humanism
Humanism is not a religion and Humanists do not believe in a god or gods. They do not have a higher authority or tradition to turn to for help and guidance on how they should live their lives. They believe that humans must take responsibility for their own lives and see their individual conscience as a source of authority.

### Jainism
Because Jains do not believe in a god in the traditional sense they find authority in the examples of the lives of the Tirthankaras, the scriptures and senior ascetics.

### Zoroastrianism
Zoroastrians find authority in the teachings of Zoroaster, their prophet, and in their belief in the one true God, Ahura Mazda ('Wise Lord').

# Drawing it all together

## Learning about religion

1 Compare the way in which Christians think about authority with the views on authority of one of the other religions you have studied.

2 Write a paragraph using the following terms and show that you understand them:

  **believers**

  **bishop.**

## Learning from religion

1 Make two lists. In one put all the good things you can think of about authority and in the other the things that you do not like about it. Look at which list has the most in it and write a couple of sentences saying why.

**Hint** In writing your lists you need to think about how authority affects you and also other people.

2 'People need to have authority in their lives so that they know what to do.' Discuss this statement with a partner and share your opinions.

**Hint** You might want to think about how authority can affect people's lives and whether it is more than all good or all bad.

3 People such as teachers and the police have authority. Write down as many ways as you can think of in which the type of authority they hold might be different from religious authority.

**Hint** You may find that in some ways these types of authority are the same and if so you should comment on this.

# 1.1 What makes a good leader?

## Your lesson objectives

**In this lesson you will:**

- think about what makes a good leader

- decide whether religious leaders need different qualities from other leaders

- understand that some leaders have charisma.

## Your key words

**charisma**

a natural ability to inspire others

## Leaders and authority

In order to be able to do their job properly, it is important that leaders have some authority over the people they lead. People who do not respect the authority of their leaders will be more difficult to lead. Earning people's respect is not always easy and some less successful leaders never quite manage it.

Pável Pardo Segura, VfB Stuttgart. A leader must have qualities that other members of their team may not have. Can you name three of these qualities?

## Qualities of leadership

It is important that leaders have certain qualities. The captain of a sports team is not always the best player, but in order to be successful they must have qualities that other members of their team may not have.

The leadership qualities needed will vary. For example, while religious leaders and teachers may share similar qualities, these are quite different from the qualities needed by the boss of a large company, whose job may involve making bigger and bigger profits.

Regardless of who or what a person is leading, they have a responsibility to look after the people they lead and make sure they come to no harm. Good leaders show care, and provide support and guidance, which usually makes people happy to be led.

The very best leaders have **charisma**: something extra that inspires people to listen to and respect them. This cannot be taught or learnt, but it helps a person to influence or attract others without even seeming to try.

Some say that this is a quality God gives to some people to help them use their talents effectively. Others say it is a natural part of some people's characters and that God has nothing to do with it. Whichever is correct, charisma certainly helps some leaders to stand out from others and exercise their authority easily and successfully.

## Learning about religion

1 Explain the meaning of 'charisma'.

2 Why do you think leaders with charisma seem to be more successful than leaders without it?

3 Try to think of a person who has charisma. Explain how their charisma helps this person to do their work.

## Your discussion

What do you think a leader can do to earn the respect of the people they are leading?

# 1.1 What makes a good leader?

### Bahá'í
In 1863, Bahá'u'lláh announced that he had a divine mission as a messenger of God. Bahá'ís admire him for his faith and his courage in his lifetime.

### Hinduism
Hinduism does not have a centralised leadership structure and there are different types of leaders. They include ancient sages (wise men), warrior kings, mystics, saints, scholars and founders of key lines of descent. Priests mainly come from the brahmin class, who traditionally were highly respected for their learning and wisdom.

### Islam
A Muslim prayer leader is called an *imam* and is chosen by the local community. He must have an in-depth knowledge and understanding of Islam. His opinion is respected by Muslims because of his learning.

### Judaism
In the Jewish community, leaders are called *rabbi*s. A *rabbi* has a very good understanding of Jewish law and is able to use it to answer any questions people may have. *Rabbi*s lead worship and guide and advise Jews within the community.

### Buddhism
His Holiness the 14th Dalai Lama is both the civil and the spiritual leader of the Tibetan people and is respected by Buddhists across the world, in particular as a worker for peace and for his humility (humbleness).

### Humanism
Humanists consider that a leadership role is a very serious undertaking. When someone is given authority they have the right to expect obedience and the power to enforce it. Power brings responsibility and all leaders have a responsibility for the people they lead.

### Jainism
Leadership within Jainism is seen to have come from 24 Tirthankaras or Jinas. They are spiritual leaders whose teachings form the basis of the religion. They are respected as liberated souls who practised perfect discipline and have infinite knowledge.

### Sikhism
Sikhs believe that the Guru Granth Sahib Ji is the word of God, written by some of the *guru*s who were inspired by God. It has taken the place of a human *guru* and is treated with enormous respect.

### Zoroastrianism
Zoroastrianism is named after a man called Zoroaster, a prophet and priest who spent many years travelling and searching for the truth about God.

# Drawing it all together

## Learning about religion

**1** Using two of the religions you have studied compare what they believe about what makes a good leader.

**2** Write a paragraph using the following terms and show that you understand them:

**leadership**

**respect**

**responsibility.**

## Learning from religion

**1** What do you think are the most important qualities for leadership?

**Hint** Think about why you might decide to do what someone else tells you.

**2** How do you think a religious follower might decide what is important to follow in their faith and what is not?

**Hint** You need to consider whether people might decide to follow a particular book or perhaps what a living person says to them. You also need to think whether they might say that everything is equally important to them.

**3** 'Rather than thinking that having people in authority over us is stopping us from doing what we want to do, perhaps we should think of it as stopping others from doing things that may hurt us.'

Spend a minute thinking about the sentence above and then discuss your thoughts with a partner.

**Hint** Make sure that you balance your argument carefully when deciding whether you agree with this or not.

# 1.2 Is God the leader?

In the last lesson you looked at the qualities good leaders need, and you may have felt that you have some of these qualities. Many religious people who also possess these qualities believe that there is another important factor that helps them in their lives.

Christians believe that, after God created the earth, he went on to be involved with everything that happens in the world. They argue that if this were not the case, God's role in creation would be rather pointless.

Christians believe that God influences what happens on earth by working through people who try to make life better. He may help them to make decisions or give them strength or protection to make their work easier. For example, a doctor who is a Christian may believe that their job as a doctor is a **vocation** and that God has given them the ability to do it well. They may decide to use their skills to help people in need. They feel they are doing the work that God wants them to and that he is with them, guiding and protecting them.

## Your lesson objectives

**In this lesson you will:**

- evaluate whether God can inspire people to do things
- consider God's influence on religious leaders in the Christian Church.

## Your key words

**community**

a group of people who share something in common

**ordination**

the act of admitting a priest to the ministry

**vocation**

a feeling that someone is 'called' to follow a certain career, possibly by God

## Leaders of religions

Christians expect their leaders (priests, bishops, ministers) to have more of God's qualities than some other people do. This is especially important to them because if they ask for advice and help from a priest, they expect this to be the advice that God would give.

When people become priests, they believe that they are given special authority from God. They have a ceremony of **ordination** at the end of their training to become a priest. At this ceremony, the Christian **community** confirms that this person should become a priest.

You have a vocation from God.

If you already know what it is, pray to be faithful.

If you are still searching, pray to hear God's voice and to respond generously.

(A Church of England prayer for vocation)

It is believed that once they have been ordained priests are able to act 'in the person of Christ'.

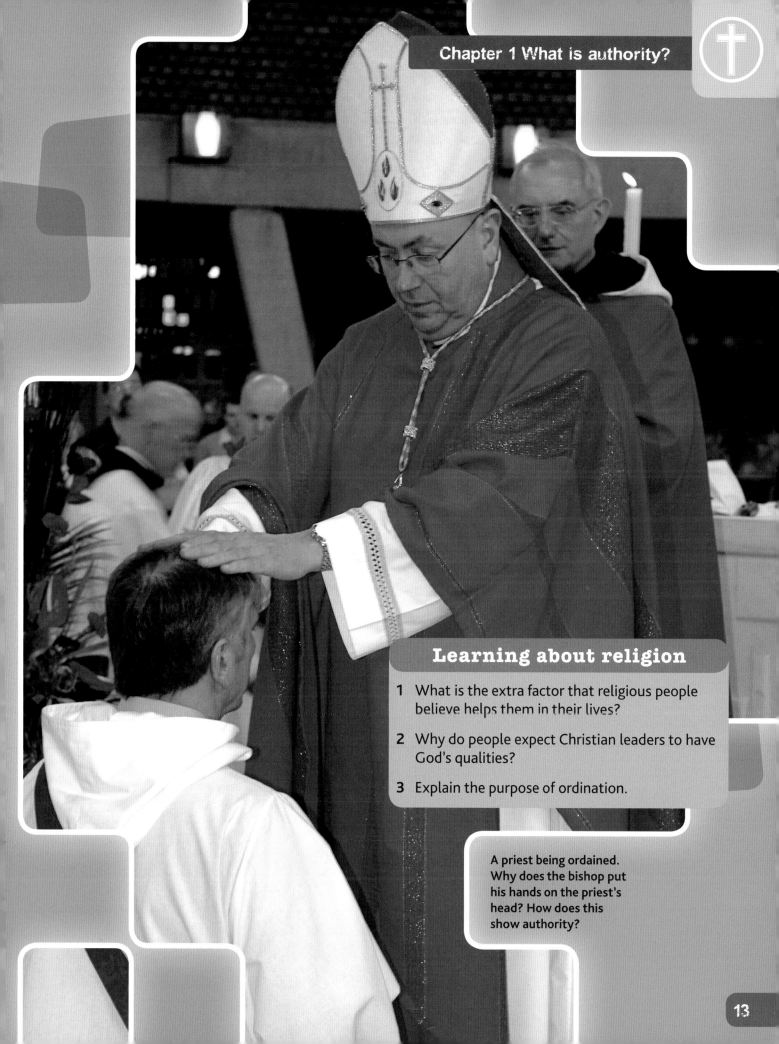

## Learning about religion

1 What is the extra factor that religious people believe helps them in their lives?

2 Why do people expect Christian leaders to have God's qualities?

3 Explain the purpose of ordination.

A priest being ordained. Why does the bishop put his hands on the priest's head? How does this show authority?

# 1.2 Is God the leader?

### Bahá'í
Bahá'ís believe there are two levels of leadership based on agreements or Covenants. The Lesser Covenant was made between followers and Bahá'u'lláh, God's manifestation. The Greater Covenant is between God and the whole of humanity.

### Buddhism
Buddhists do not believe in a supreme creator god. Instead they try to find the truth about life from within themselves and by seeking to reach enlightenment. They also follow the teachings and example of earthly leaders such as the Dalai Lama.

### Hinduism
Hindus believe that all leaders get their power, vision and influence from God, the ultimate leader. He guides all humans from within, as the source of all ability, intelligence and inspiration.

### Humanism
Humanists do not believe in a god or gods. There are no leaders and no special books to tell them what to believe or how to behave. They believe that it is the responsibility of every individual to make decisions for themselves.

### Islam
Muslims believe that: 'There is no god but Allah; Muhammad 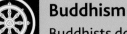 is the messenger of Allah.' Allah has great authority over his followers. Nothing or no one is Allah's equal and images, statues and pictures of him are forbidden.

### Jainism
Jains do not believe in a god in the traditional sense. They believe that there are divine beings worthy of devotion, but much of the religion of Jainism is about the individual and their journey to try to achieve liberation.

### Judaism
One of the most important prayers in Judaism is the Shema. This stresses that there is one God and he should be respected: 'Hear, O Israel, the Lord is our G-d, the Lord is one.'

### Sikhism
Sikh beliefs about God are found at the beginning of the Guru Granth Sahib Ji in a prayer known as the Mool Mantar. It starts with the statement: 'One Universal Creator God./ The Name Is Truth.'

### Zoroastrianism
Zoroastrians believe that there is one true God, Ahura Mazda ('Wise Lord'). He is the creator of the world and knows everything that happens in it. Zoroastrians praise him and worship him.

# Drawing it all together

## Learning about religion

1 For two of the religions which you have studied make a list showing what they believe about God being their leader. Compare your lists with a partner.

2 Write a definition of these words:

ministry

priest.

## Learning from religion

1 Consider whether, if people believe that God is their leader, they also need priests or other religious leaders.

**Hint** You need to think carefully about the role of human religious leaders and what they may do that other people do not.

2 'If people have strong human leaders then they do not need a god to tell them what to do.' Discuss this statement with a partner and share your opinions.

**Hint** Remember that just because someone is a strong leader it does not necessarily mean that they are a good one.

3 How might believing that God is the most important leader affect the way in which someone lives?

**Hint** You need to consider the way in which people treat each other as well as how they might worship God.

# 1.3 God on earth

## Your lesson objectives

**In this lesson you will:**

- understand that Christians believe God came to earth in the form of Jesus

- evaluate whether this is important for human beings.

## Your key words

**belief**

accepting that something is true or real

**crucified**

fastened to a cross and left to die – a form of execution used by the Romans

**Heaven**

a place of paradise and reward in the presence of God

**Messiah**

'anointed one', a spiritual leader sent by God to help people on earth return to God's laws

**prophet**

someone who receives a message or inspiration from God

**resurrected**

raised from the dead

**virgin**

a person who has not had sex

## What Christians believe about God on earth

Most of the main religions teach that God has made himself known by inspiring either leaders or writers of holy books. The advice contained in the holy books helps believers to live the sort of life they think God wants them to.

Christians take this further because they believe that God actually came to earth as a man, Jesus of Nazareth. They believe he was the **Messiah**, someone sent by God to help people on earth as their Saviour. (The Messiah is expected by the Jews, but Jews do not believe that Jesus was the Messiah, although they do acknowledge his existence and that he did good things.)

Christians tend to refer to Jesus as the 'Son of God' rather than God or the Messiah. This does not alter their **belief** that he was God in human form and the Messiah. Muslims believe that Jesus was a **prophet** (not God) and less important than Muhammad ﷺ to whom God revealed his teachings.

Christians believe that Jesus was born about 2000 years ago in Bethlehem, Palestine, the country which is now called Israel. It is said that his mother Mary was a **virgin** when she conceived Jesus – this belief is very important, especially to Roman Catholics, and shows the uniqueness of Jesus. After being **baptised** by his cousin John the Baptist, Jesus taught people a new way of living, worked miracles and at the age of around 32 or 33 was arrested, tried and **crucified** in Jerusalem by the Romans. The Romans had invaded Palestine in 63 BCE and made the country part of their empire for more than 400 years.

On the third day after he was crucified, Jesus' tomb was found to be empty. This has led Christians to believe that he was **resurrected** (raised from the dead) and that they could be united with God after death by committing themselves to him and following his teachings. After being seen by some of his followers, he left them for the last time; Christians believe he returned to **Heaven**.

Christians believe Jesus was crucified for teaching a new way of living. What do the gospels say happened next?

## How important are Christian beliefs?

If God did come to earth in the form of a man, Jesus of Nazareth, it means that the teachings of Christianity are very powerful because they are from God and have his authority.

## Learning about religion

1 Make an ideas map to show what you know about the life and death of Jesus.

2 Why do people think that Jesus was God on earth? Explain your answer.

# 1.3 God on earth

## Bahá'í
Bahá'u'lláh and his predecessor the Báb were manifestations of God and received revelations from God. However, Bahá'ís do not believe that God comes to earth.

## Buddhism
Buddhists do not believe in a supreme creator god. Although the Buddha lived on the earth and spread his teachings they do not believe he was a god.

## Hinduism
Hindus believe that God periodically descends to earth to protect devout believers, destroy evil and re-establish religious principles. Most important examples of this are the ten avatars (descents) of Vishnu, especially Lord Rama and Lord Krishna.

## Humanism
Humanism is not a religion and Humanists do not believe in a god or gods. Therefore they do not believe that a god can come to earth.

## Islam
Muslims believe that all authority comes from the one God, Allah. However, although they believe that Muhammad ﷺ was God's messenger on earth they do not believe that Allah would ever come to earth.

## Jainism
Jains believe that there have been 24 Tirthankaras on earth who have established the Jain religion.

## Judaism
Jews do not believe that G-d would come to earth and, although they are waiting for a Messiah, they do not believe that he will be a god.

## Sikhism
Sikhs do not believe in a physical god who would come to earth.

## Zoroastrianism
Zoroastrians believe that God, Ahura Mazda, is all good and that he created the world, which is therefore also good. All misery, disease, suffering and death come from the evil one, Angra Mainyu. They believe in revelation and that evil comes to earth and causes suffering.

# Drawing it all together

## Learning about religion

1 From the religions which you have studied choose two with different beliefs about whether God comes to earth. Explain the view of each of these.

2 Write a paragraph using the following terms and show that you understand them:

   **miracle**

   **Son of God.**

## Learning from religion

1 Choose a religion which you have studied whose followers believe that God does appear on earth. Write a passage explaining how you think both followers of this religion and others might react to this happening.

**Hint** Remember that you need to include the views of believers and others. Also, not all believers might react in the same way.

2 'God should come to earth to help when so many people are suffering.' Discuss this statement with a partner and share your opinions.

**Hint** You might want to think about how people would expect God to help if he did appear on earth.

3 Can you think of a world that could be the best of all possible worlds? What would it be like?

**Hint** Think carefully of the results of what you have chosen.

# 1.4 Why are sacred writings special?

## Your lesson objectives

**In this lesson you will:**

- understand why sacred writings are important
- learn more about the Bible
- evaluate whether sacred writings have anything to say to people today.

You have already discovered that some religious people believe that God influences how they live by inspiring certain people to write down his teachings. These **sacred writings** are of great importance to religious believers. As written texts, they are not going to change (although their language may be translated or updated) and in case of disagreement, people can check them. The spoken word is different – once something has been said, it may be remembered inaccurately or lost.

## Your key words

**faith**

belief in somebody or something especially without logical proof

**gospels**

the first four books in the New Testament

**sacred writings**

texts that are important and special to religious people as they tell them about their faith and which they believe to have been inspired by God

**Ten Commandments**

a set of rules given by God to Moses, which Jews and Christians try to follow in their lives

## The Bible

The sacred writings of Christianity are found in the Bible. The Bible consists of two sections or testaments: the Old Testament, which was written before the time of Jesus, and the New Testament, which was probably mostly written in the first century CE. The Old Testament contains the same books as the Tenakh, the sacred writings of the Jews. Christians believe the Old Testament is important because it contains God's rules on how to live (such as the **Ten Commandments**) and how to prepare for the coming of the Messiah. Some parts of it, such as the Psalms, are used in Christian worship. The writers of the Old Testament had great wisdom and **faith** in God's authority, and their inspiration influenced their writings and made them special. The New Testament is about Jesus and the first Christians.

Both testaments contain sections called 'books'. The first four books of the New Testament are called **gospels** (which means 'good news'). They were written by four people who are traditionally called Matthew, Mark, Luke and John. Possibly the writers never met Jesus themselves but wrote down what people were saying about him. Christians believe that these accounts of Jesus' life and teaching were inspired by God. The rest of the New Testament tells of the start of the Christian Church, focusing on the contribution of St Paul, who worked hard to spread the new faith. It contains epistles (letters) to the new Churches as well as the Acts of the Apostles and Revelation.

ACCORDING

JOHN

**The Bible.**

IN the *b*beginning was the Word, and the *c*Word was with God, and the *d*Word was *e*God.

2 The same was in the *a*beginning with God.

3 All things were *a*made by him; and without him was not any thing made that was made.

## How are sacred writings used today?

Sacred writings are very special to religious believers because they are often written by important people in each faith and are thought to be one of God's main ways of communicating with people. They focus on what their authors considered to be important many years ago. However, all sacred writings contain eternal truths that are relevant to the 21st century, even though life was very different when they were written.

## Learning about religion

1 Name two sacred writings.

2 Explain in detail the main differences between the Old Testament and the New Testament.

3 Why do many people think that sacred writings are important?

# 1.4 Why are sacred writings special?

## Bahá'í
The sacred writings of the Bahá'í faith are by Bahá'u'lláh. Some of his most important works are the 'Book of Certitude', which shows the common origins of the world's religions, the 'Hidden Words', which contains the common truths of these religions and the 'Most Holy Book'.

## Hinduism
The two types of sacred teaching are the *Shruti* ('that which is heard'), which were revealed by God to ancient sages, and the more recent *Smriti* ('that which is remembered'), which help make the *Shruti* more accessible, often through story.

## Jainism
Some Jain scriptures contain the key teachings of Mahavira who was the 24th Tirthankara and achieved liberation. The aim of all Jains is to follow his example and they believe this can be achieved through following his teachings.

## Sikhism
The Guru Granth Sahib Ji, the sacred writing of Sikhs, is seen as the final *guru*, and includes many of the words and teachings of the nine human *guru*s. This makes it special because it is seen to have the authority of God.

## Buddhism
Theravada Buddhists believe that their most important sacred writings are the Tipitaka/Tripitaka, the 'Three Baskets'. These contain teachings from the Buddha himself together with rules for monks and include the Four Noble Truths and the Noble Eightfold Path.

## Humanism
As Humanism is not a religion it does not have any writings which are thought of as sacred.

## Islam
The Qur'an is thought to be the actual words of Allah as given to Muhammad ﷺ which were later written down in Arabic with total accuracy.

## Judaism
The main sacred text for Jews is called the Torah which means 'law' or 'teaching'. Orthodox Jews believe that the Torah is the actual word of G-d revealed to Moses.

## Zoroastrianism
In Zoroastrianism, the most sacred texts are the Avesta and the Gathas. The Avesta is a collection of important writings that have been brought together over thousands of years. The Gathas contain 17 hymns written by Zoroaster.

# Drawing it all together

## Learning about religion

1 Looking at two of the religions which you have studied, write down what is the same and what is different in what people believe about their sacred texts.

2 Write a definition of these words:

revelation

testament.

## Learning from religion

1 Choose a religion where most followers believe that their sacred text is the actual word of God. Explain how you think believers would be influenced by this.

**Hint** Remember that this can include how this might affect people's lives as well as their beliefs.

2 Imagine that you are about to start a new religion. Write a passage explaining what you might take as being a sacred text and why.

**Hint** Remember to think about the content of the text you are choosing. You need to explain why you have chosen it and why you think it is important.

3 'Sacred texts are much too old to mean anything to people today.' Discuss this statement with a partner and share your opinions.

**Hint** You might want to think about how people would expect God to help if he did appear on earth.

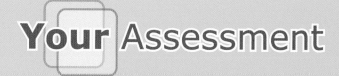

# Your Assessment

Make a list of the different types of authority you have looked at in this chapter. Explain why you think some forms of religious authority are more important than others.

**Hint** Remember to look at different religious views as well as non-religious ones.

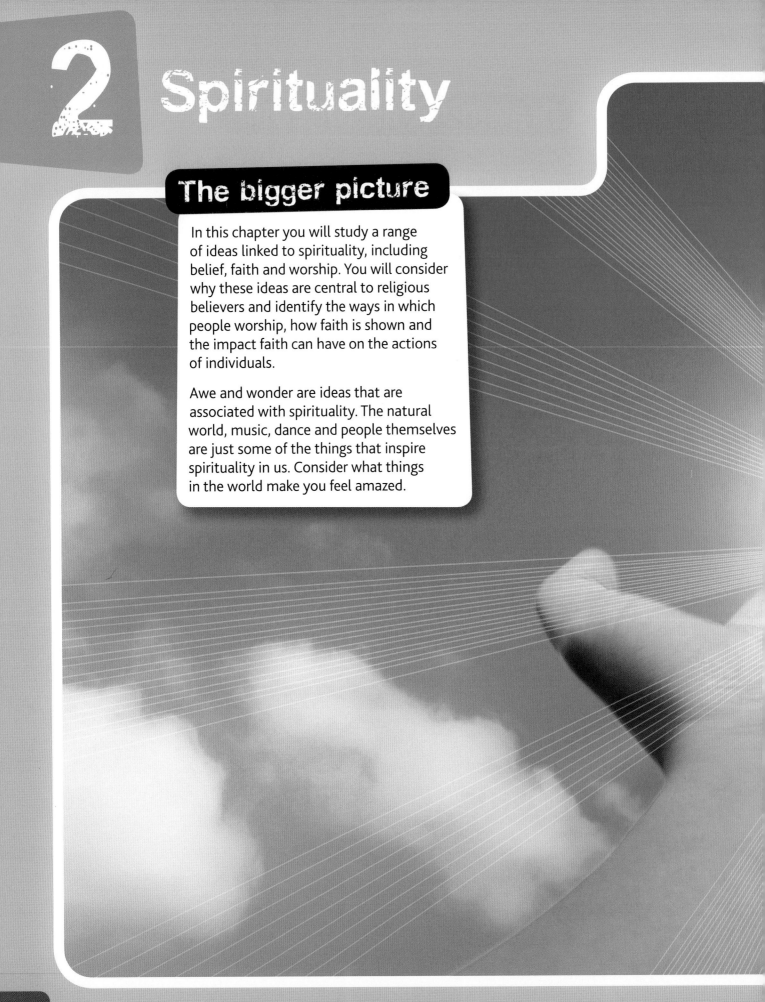

# 2 Spirituality

## The bigger picture

In this chapter you will study a range of ideas linked to spirituality, including belief, faith and worship. You will consider why these ideas are central to religious believers and identify the ways in which people worship, how faith is shown and the impact faith can have on the actions of individuals.

Awe and wonder are ideas that are associated with spirituality. The natural world, music, dance and people themselves are just some of the things that inspire spirituality in us. Consider what things in the world make you feel amazed.

## Learning about religion

Make a list of ideas to describe 'spirituality'. Compare your ideas with a partner – which ideas are the same and which are different?

## Your discussion

Do you think spirituality and religion are the same thing? Explain the reasons for your view.

# 2 Introduction

# What is worship?

## Your lesson objectives

**In this lesson you will:**

- explore what the term 'worship' means
- investigate the importance of worship for religious believers
- consider what worship means to Christians.

## Your key words

**belief**

accepting that something is true or real

**Bible**

a word used for the sacred writings of the Jews (Tenakh) and Christians (Old and New Testaments)

**commitment**

a sense of being dedicated to something

**community**

a group of people who share something in common

**denomination**

a branch of a religion

**devotion**

loving or being dedicated to something or someone

**evidence**

facts that can be used as proof

## What does the term 'worship' mean?

The term '**worship**' is used in many contexts, but it is most commonly associated with religion. There is **evidence** that people have worshipped gods, their surroundings, leaders and other humans for thousands of years.

Today, people may think that celebrities are 'worshipped', as people are influenced by them and inspired to act, dress or behave like them.

Worship can also be associated with places or objects; an individual may be inspired by a particular building or image that they feel is significant and meaningful. The way they respond to these things or act towards them is similar to the **commitment** and **devotion** often seen in religious worship.

Candles and light are often used to create atmosphere and mood. How may they be used in worship? Why do you think this may be important?

## What does worship mean in terms of religion and why is it important?

Worship is important to religion. Many religious believers express themselves through worship or use acts of worship to show commitment and devotion towards God. Worship can take place in holy buildings, at home or outside, and may be done individually or in a group with others, giving a sense of **community.**

Worship practices differ from religion to religion, and also within religions, because of different interpretations or understandings of the **faith**. However, many acts of worship have some common features, for example prayer, meditation, offerings, reading **sacred writings** or living in the way each religion accepts.

Worship is a form of devotion and reflection which can unite people and provide a feeling of identity and belonging. Worship can also give comfort, hope and a feeling that a person is living according to their faith.

## Your key words

**faith**

belief in somebody or something especially without logical proof

**sacred writings**

texts that are important and special to religious people as they tell them about their faith and which they believe to have been inspired by God

**worship**

to show love, respect or devotion to someone or something

# What does worship mean to Christians?

Worship is important as it is a sign of Christian **belief**. All Christians worship one God, but the way in which people worship varies from one **denomination** to another. Prayers, sermons, music, and readings from the **Bible** all feature in Christian worship. Some Christians believe that helping others who are in need and treating others the way Jesus treated people is a form of worshipping God, as they are putting his teachings into action in the world. Many Christians will choose to attend a place of worship and practise their faith with others to gain a sense of community and shared support and because they believe that God calls them to do so.

## Learning about religion

1 Explain in your own words what you understand the term 'worship' to mean.

2 Think of a hobby or activity that you enjoy doing. What similarities and differences are there between the commitment you show to this and the worship of religious believers?

3 Create an ideas map showing reasons why worship is important to religious believers.

# 2 Introduction
# What is worship?

## Bahá'í
Most Bahá'í meetings are held in individuals' homes, local Bahá'í centres or rented accommodation. Across the world, there are currently seven Bahá'í Houses of Worship (temples).

## Hinduism
Worship is mainly directed toward God, or his natural representatives, such as elders, the *gurus*, the many gods and goddesses and even the special features of nature. Worship is primarily a means of loving exchange between the individual and God.

## Islam
Prayer is the main form of worship in Islam. One of the duties of Muslims is to pray five times a day at set times. There is a communal service on a Friday for special prayers and a sermon is given by an *imam*.

## Judaism
Prayer is the key feature of Jewish worship and usually Jews will pray three times a day – at morning, noon and night. Jewish communal worship usually takes place in a synagogue.

## Buddhism
Buddhism does not believe in a creator god so followers do not worship a supreme being. Instead, they show respect towards the Buddha and follow his example to better themselves. Sacred prayers are recited and *mantras* repeated.

## Humanism
As Humanists do not believe in God they do not have forms of worship.

## Jainism
Worship is important in Jainism but can take different forms. It can be the quiet repetition of a *mantra* or chant or more elaborate *puja* where images are decorated for a ceremonial ritual.

## Sikhism
Sikhs worship in a *gurdwara*. Their form of worship usually involves singing hymns and listening to a reading from the Guru Granth Sahib Ji.

## Zoroastrianism
Zoroastrian worship is prayer. Zoroastrians can pray anywhere where they are facing God's creation: fire, light or water. Wherever possible they will worship in front of the fire in a fire temple. The *sudre kusti* prayers are the main form of daily worship.

# Drawing it all together

## Learning about religion

1 Looking at two of the religions which you have studied, make two lists showing the main points about their worship.

2 Write a definition of these words:

meditation

offering.

## Learning from religion

1 Although followers of different religions may worship in different ways there may be similarities in their forms of worship. Identify two areas that are similar in the religions you are studying and explain why they are important to people.

**Hint** Remember to think about how these parts of their worship might affect people's lives as well as showing their beliefs.

2 Imagine that you have to think of a new way of worship for a religion. Write a passage explaining what this might be and why.

**Hint** This should be something that people do not already do and that would help them feel closer to their faith.

3 'The most important way to worship is just by living your life well.' Discuss this statement with a partner and share your opinions.

**Hint** You need to think about how living a life well might be a form of worship and whether there are parts of worship that need more than this.

# 2.1 What is belief – truth or myth?

## Your lesson objectives

**In this lesson you will:**

- consider what belief is
- investigate the difference between belief, fact and opinion
- explore the importance of belief to faith.

## What is belief?

A belief is something that a person holds to be true but which cannot necessarily be proved to be true. Everyone has beliefs and different people have different beliefs as a result of their upbringing or individual experiences. This will lead them to value different things. For example, Christians believe that God exists, which affects how they lead their lives, how they spend their time and how they behave towards others.

## Your key words

**fact**

something that can be proved to be true

**myth**

a story which is used to describe an important belief using language that is colourful or relates to the supernatural

**opinion**

someone's personal view on a subject

**proof**

evidence that something is true or exists

**prophecy**

a prediction of the future, believed to come from God

**supernatural**

something thought to be the result of a force beyond scientific understanding or the laws of nature

## What is the difference between belief, fact and opinion?

Belief, **fact** and **opinion** are closely related. Look at the examples of belief, fact and opinion below. How are they the same? How are they different?

| | |
|---|---|
| | **Belief** |
| | I believe in God. |
| | **Fact** |
| | There are 66 books in the Bible. |
| | **Opinion** |
| | In my opinion you do not have to be in a place of worship to pray to God. |

A German translation of the Bible. Christians believe the Bible is the word of God. They put their faith in it and use it for guidance and answers when they need help. Christians base their lives on it. What or who do you put your faith in and why?

30

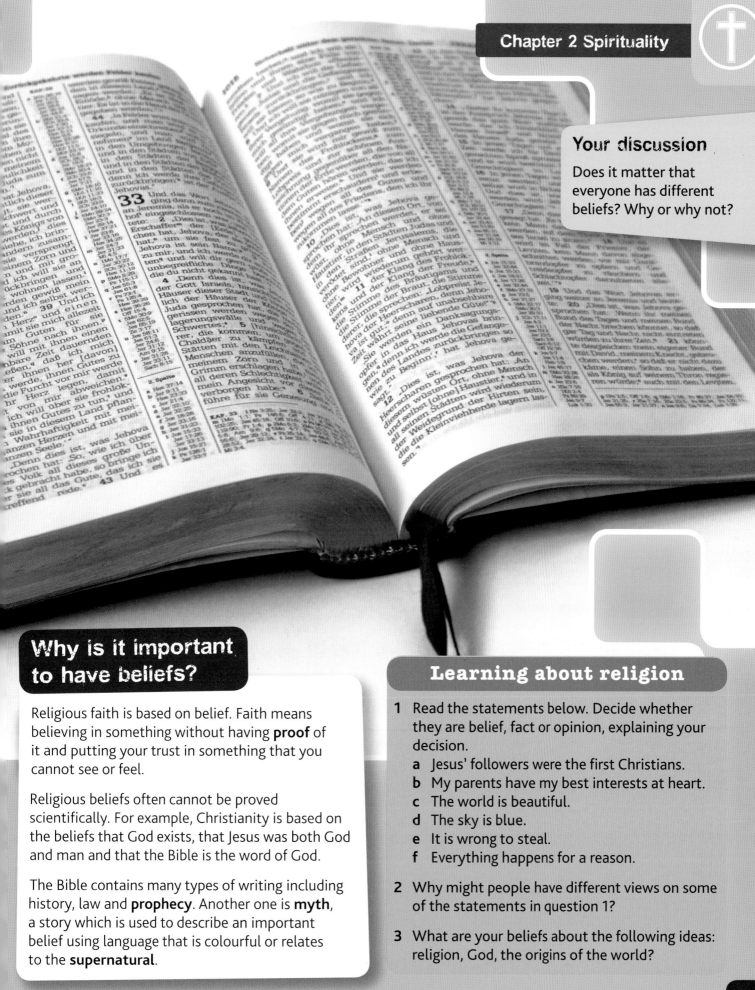

## Your discussion

Does it matter that everyone has different beliefs? Why or why not?

# Why is it important to have beliefs?

Religious faith is based on belief. Faith means believing in something without having **proof** of it and putting your trust in something that you cannot see or feel.

Religious beliefs often cannot be proved scientifically. For example, Christianity is based on the beliefs that God exists, that Jesus was both God and man and that the Bible is the word of God.

The Bible contains many types of writing including history, law and **prophecy**. Another one is **myth**, a story which is used to describe an important belief using language that is colourful or relates to the **supernatural**.

# Learning about religion

1 Read the statements below. Decide whether they are belief, fact or opinion, explaining your decision.
   a Jesus' followers were the first Christians.
   b My parents have my best interests at heart.
   c The world is beautiful.
   d The sky is blue.
   e It is wrong to steal.
   f Everything happens for a reason.

2 Why might people have different views on some of the statements in question 1?

3 What are your beliefs about the following ideas: religion, God, the origins of the world?

# 2.1 What is belief – truth or myth?

**Bahá'í**
Bahá'ís accept the teachings of most of the world's religions as the truth and believe that their founders explained God's will to people.

**Buddhism**
Buddhism is often viewed as a philosophy, rather than a religion, as followers do not worship a god but follow the Buddha, who is identified as a spiritual guide.

**Hinduism**
For Hindus, beliefs are different ways of seeing the same truth. Hindu philosophy and theology discuss three main concepts: the self, matter and God.

**Humanism**
Humanists believe that the only sources of knowledge and moral codes to live by are human experience and rational thinking. They believe that truth can only be discovered through using reason and evidence.

**Islam**
Belief is at the centre of Islam and forms the foundations on which the religion is based. The Five Pillars are the core duties that every Muslim has to perform.

**Jainism**
Belief is important to Jainism. The Tirthankaras brought together many new ideas and Jains need to put their faith in these in order to practise their religion.

**Judaism**
The key beliefs in Judaism unite all believers as a global community and they can be seen as ultimate truths of the faith.

**Sikhism**
For Sikhism, belief is viewed as truth. These beliefs cannot be challenged or changed as they are the foundations on which the teachings of the faith are established.

**Zoroastrianism**
In a religion as old as Zoroastrianism there are many different beliefs and ways in which people understand these. Some people believe that practice is the most important part of their religion whilst others are particularly concerned about the stories or myths on which it is based. The Gathas are particularly important.

# Drawing it all together

## Learning about religion

1  For two of the religions you have studied compare what they teach about what is truth.

2  Write a paragraph using the following terms and show that you understand them:

  **faith**

  **value.**

## Learning from religion

1  Using examples from religions you have studied explain the importance of belief.

**Hint** In your answer think about what people believe and how important these beliefs are to them.

2  How might you tell whether a story is factually true or a myth which contains 'truths' about human life and experience? Try to give examples.

**Hint** You might begin by looking at Genesis in the Bible.

3  'Facts are always more important than beliefs.' Discuss this statement with a partner and share your opinions.

**Hint** You need to think about what facts and beliefs contribute to a faith.

# 2.2 What do people believe?

## Your lesson objectives

**In this lesson you will:**

- investigate what Christians believe

- explain how Christian beliefs are put into action

- reflect on the importance of Christian beliefs in the world today.

## Your key words

**creed**
a statement of belief

**crucified**
fastened to a cross and left to die – a form of execution used by the Romans

**Holy Spirit**
one person of the Trinity, the other two being the Father and the Son

**monotheistic**
believing in one god

**resurrected**
raised from the dead

**scriptures**
holy or sacred writings

## What do Christians believe?

Christianity is thought to be the largest religion in the world today, with over two billion followers. All Christians are united under the heading of 'Christianity', but there are many denominations within this religion which interpret and practise their faith differently. However, there are a number of core beliefs that all Christians share.

Christianity is a **monotheistic** religion which means followers believe in one God. God is all-powerful and the creator of the world. Christians call him 'Father'.

In Christianity, there are **creeds** which state the main beliefs. The main creeds are the Nicene Creed and the Apostles' Creed.

The Holy Bible is the Christian **scripture**. It contains stories about the faith, the **Ten Commandments**, and information about the life, death and resurrection of Jesus of Nazareth.

Christians believe that God sent his son Jesus Christ to earth to teach people the way of God. He is an example for people to follow. Jesus was **crucified** and **resurrected** showing people the way to Heaven.

The **Trinity** is a Christian idea. This is the belief in God being the Father, the Son and the Holy Spirit.

## How are Christian beliefs put into action?

Different denominations of Christians practise their faith in different ways, but all recognise the basic beliefs of the faith as important. This means that they will try to live in a good way, following the example of Jesus. They will follow the teachings of the Bible and of the creeds and try to be good Christians.

They believe that God wants them to be like Jesus and, with the help of the **Holy Spirit**, to help people who are suffering in society. Some may campaign or carry out charity work, while others may feel a duty to share their faith with other people.

## Your key words

**Ten Commandments**
a set of rules given by God to Moses, which Jews and Christians try to follow in their lives

**Trinity**
the mystery of one God in three persons: Father, Son and Holy Spirit

Jesus has traditionally been represented as white but some Christians in countries such as Africa and America have begun to represent Jesus in a way that is easier for them to identify with. This 1998 painting of the Virgin Mary and Jesus, *Black Madonna III (Classic)* by Elizabeth Barakah Hodges, is one example.

## Learning about religion

1   Draw an image to represent each of the Christian beliefs summarised in the blue speech bubbles.

2   Explain the link between believing something and acting in a particular way. Try to give two examples of this within your life and two from the life of a Christian (choose two different ones if you are a Christian yourself).

3   Create a quiz on the theme of 'Christian beliefs'. Exchange it with a partner and see if you can solve the answers.

## How relevant are Christian beliefs in the world today?

Christian beliefs are widely seen in society today, both within the laws of many countries and in the way which people behave towards each other. Many other religions teach similar rules and ideas.

# 2.2 What do people believe?

### Bahá'í
Bahá'ís believe in one God who created everything and is in control of the universe. They understand that all religious teachings come from God.

### Buddhism
Buddhists do not believe in a supreme creator god. They show respect towards the Buddha and follow his example to better themselves.

### Hinduism
Hinduism has many different theologies and philosophies. However, there are ideas these have in common, such as the eternal self, *karma*, God, reincarnation and liberation.

### Humanism
Humanism is based on reason, not faith. The Humanist view of the world does not involve belief in a god or gods. Humanists may describe themselves as agnostic because they think it is impossible to know whether there is a god or not.

### Islam
The teachings of Islam revolve around two main ideas: *iman* (faith) and *ibadah* (acts). Beliefs link these ideas, as Muslims have faith in their beliefs which causes them to act in ways that please Allah.

### Jainism
Jainism does not believe in a creator god. Many Jain beliefs are focused on the soul and its liberation from the physical world.

### Judaism
An important belief of Judaism is that G-d created every person in the world in his image, meaning that all humans have the will and ability to make their own decisions.

### Sikhism
Sikhs believe in one God and accept he is the same for all people. Sikhs believe daily communication with God is necessary and that an individual relationship with God is desirable.

### Zoroastrianism
In Zoroastrianism, people believe in one God. They call this God Ahura Mazda, which means 'Wise Lord'. Zoroastrians believe that Ahura Mazda created the world.

# Drawing it all together

## Learning about religion

**1** Make a list showing the similarities and differences in the beliefs about God in two of the religions you have studied.

**2** Write a definition of these words:

**commandments**

**charity.**

## Learning from religion

**1** Explain why you think that followers of some faiths find it important to have a statement of their beliefs.

**Hint** In your answer try to give examples of some statements of belief.

**2** Do you think it is important that all members of a religion should believe the same thing? Why/why not?

**Hint** Make sure you explain your answer and try to give examples.

**3** Working with a partner, discuss what you think is the most important thing to believe in.

**Hint** Remember that you are discussing what you believe in rather than what you know.

# 2.3 Symbols and images

## What is a symbol?

The simplest definition of a **symbol** is 'an action, image, object or picture that is used to represent something else'. Symbolism is not just a religious idea; symbols are used in many non-religious situations, for example in road signs or as logos on branded products. Symbols are given great importance within many religions, as they can convey difficult ideas more easily than words.

## How are symbols used in religion?

Symbols are used as a form of language in religion, as they illustrate meaning and help with understanding. Many ideas within religion are not easy to explain in words, and symbols make these ideas clearer. For example, Christian beliefs about God are difficult to explain in words, but symbols can help Christians understand God better and relate to him on a personal level.

Images and symbols are also used as **emotive** reminders of important events. The cross is a common image within Christianity and helps Christians to remember Jesus' sacrifice.

Symbols also play a part in Christian worship. In churches, they may be used for decoration or to remind Christians about their faith. They also have a role in prayer, as images can help concentration.

1 Draw five symbols you recognise. For each one, write down its meaning and a sentence explaining why it is easy to understand the symbol.

2 Make an ideas map showing how symbols are used in religion. Use images and words.

3 Copy the Christian symbols on this page and write a few sentences to explain the meaning of each one. Research other Christian symbols and do the same.

A selection of Christian symbols. Can you say which symbol is which from the description below?

## What symbols does Christianity have?

The main symbol in Christianity is the cross. This reminds Christians that Jesus died on the cross to save humans from punishment by allowing their sins to be forgiven. An empty cross also reminds Christians that Jesus was resurrected after being crucified. The crucifix is a cross with the body of Jesus on it.

It is believed that the fish symbol was originally used when Christians were **persecuted**. The Greek word for fish, *icthus*, is made up of the initial letters of the Greek words for the elements of Christian belief: 'Jesus Christ, God's Son, Saviour'.

The dove is a common Christian symbol. It represents God's spirit, the Holy Spirit, and is a symbol of peace. After the flood described in Genesis 8 it was a dove which brought an olive branch to Noah.

The first and last letters of the Greek alphabet, *alpha* and *omega*, are used to remind Christians that God is eternal because he is both the beginning and the end.

The *Chi-Rho* consists of the first two letters of the word 'Christ' in Greek.

# 2.3 Symbols and images

### Bahá'í
The official symbol of the Bahá'í Faith is the five-pointed star, but a nine-pointed star is more often used.

### Hinduism
Of the many images and symbols used in Hinduism, the written form of the sacred syllable 'Aum' is often used to represent the tradition.

### Islam
There are no official Islamic symbols but several images or symbols have a special place in the religion. Islam is very careful about using images, as Muslims do not agree with the worship of idols and images.

### Judaism
Judaism has many different types of symbols. These are not images but actions and objects that have symbolic importance.

### Sikhism
There are a number of key symbols within Sikhism. Some are visible symbols while others may be items of clothing (for example, the Five Ks, the five items, each beginning with the letter 'k', which symbolise the Sikh faith).

### Buddhism
The eight-spoked wheel is the main symbol in Buddhism. It is associated with the idea of Buddhism being a philosophy and the wheel as steering the way through life. The eight spokes of the wheel represent the Noble Eightfold Path.

### Humanism
The Happy Human symbol was chosen by Humanists to represent their view of life. The symbol highlights the Humanist teaching that, as far as we know, we have only one life and we should contribute to that life by being happy. The best way to do this is by making other people happy.

### Jainism
The Jain symbol of the raised hand means 'stop'. It represents the idea that followers should stop and think before doing anything, in order to avoid causing any harm. In the centre of the hand is the word ahimsa or non-violence – the main principle of Jainism.

### Zoroastrianism
Fire represents the fire of creation that Zoroastrians believe brought the world into being. They believe that God is present in the sacred fire.

# Drawing it all together

## Learning about religion

1 Explain the importance of symbols and images in two of the religions you have studied.

2 Write a paragraph using the following terms and show that you understand them:

**image**

**logo.**

## Learning from religion

1 Make a list of the symbols you see at home, at school or when you are outside. Which of these do you consider are useful?

**Hint** In your explanation remember to say why you think some are useful while others are not.

2 You have been asked to design a new symbol for your RE class. When you have made it you need to explain your design.

**Hint** Your symbol needs to be eye-catching and to contain something which identifies it with your class.

3 'Symbols and images help worshippers to focus on God.' Discuss this with a partner.

**Hint** Remember that you need to look at arguments for and against this statement.

# 2.4 Where and how do people worship?

## Your lesson objectives

**In this lesson you will:**

- explore where Christian worship takes place
- debate the importance of a building for worship
- understand how Christians worship.

## Your key words

**baptism**

a ceremony which cleanses a person of Original Sin and welcomes them into the Church

**Eucharist**

a service celebrating the sacrifice of the death and resurrection of Jesus Christ, using bread and wine. This is sometimes called Holy Communion (Protestant), Liturgy (Orthodox) or Mass (Roman Catholic)

**priest**

a person with the authority to perform religious ceremonies

**private worship**

when a person worships on their own

**public worship**

when groups of people worship together

**Quaker**

a member of the Christian denomination otherwise known as the Religious Society of Friends

## Where do Christians worship?

There are many denominations in Christianity and worship can take place in different places and different ways. **Public worship** takes place in cathedrals, churches, chapels, halls and other places. The place of worship often reflects the kind of worship that happens there. However, some common elements may be seen in many Christian places of worship.

This picture shows some of the features usually found in a Roman Catholic or Anglican church. The buildings and features of other denominations may be quite different.

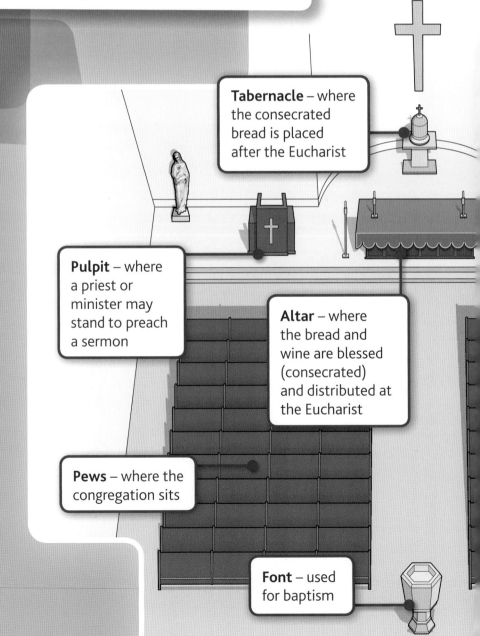

**Tabernacle** – where the consecrated bread is placed after the Eucharist

**Pulpit** – where a priest or minister may stand to preach a sermon

**Altar** – where the bread and wine are blessed (consecrated) and distributed at the Eucharist

**Pews** – where the congregation sits

**Font** – used for baptism

## How are some Christian buildings different?

The design of a church reflects the beliefs and practices of the individual denomination. For example, the Catholic, Anglican and Orthodox churches believe the **Eucharist** – the blessing and sharing of bread and wine – is very important. Their churches have the altar as the main focus. In contrast, the Free Churches believe that the word of God is most important, so the building is centred on the pulpit. In an Orthodox church, each aspect of the building is symbolically important.

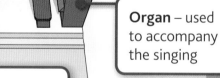

**Organ** – used to accompany the singing

**Lectern** – where the Bible is kept and read from

## How do Christians worship?

Many Christians attend church on a Sunday, their holy day, so they can pray and share faith with others, but Christians can also pray alone in **private worship**. The form a service takes varies according to the denomination. Some Christians, such as the **Quakers**, have silence and long periods of reflection in their services, while others such as Pentecostal Christians may have singing and dancing. There are, however, a number of elements of worship which many Christians share:

- prayer – a form of communication with God when believers can ask for help and guidance or offer thanks and express their love for him
- music – hymns or religious songs praising God
- **priest**/vicar/minister – the person who leads the service
- sermon/talk/homily – this explains a key theme, giving a message and interpreting the Bible reading
- Eucharist – believers share the wine and bread that represent the body and blood of Jesus Christ
- Bible readings – reflect an important message from God
- fellowship – sharing the experience of worship with other Christians
- money – a collection is made, with the money helping fund the work of the Church, to pay the clergy and maintain the building.

## Learning about religion

1  Why are all Christian places of worship not the same? Give at least one example to explain your answer.

2  What do you think the most important part of a typical church is? Give at least two reasons for your answer.

3  Create an ideas map of images and words to show the key aspects of Christian worship.

## Your discussion

'Christians do not need a special building for worship. They can pray anywhere!' What are your veiws on this statement?

# 2.4 Where and how do people worship?

### Bahá'í
Bahá'u'lláh asked his followers to choose one of three prayers to recite each day. The shortest of these prayers is just three sentences long.

### Buddhism
Some Buddhists will go to a temple to show devotion and honour the Buddha. This devotion may take the form of meditation. Many others may show devotion alone at home.

### Hinduism
Hindus worship at home, in the temple and at outdoor shrines, usually by offering articles that are associated with good fortune, such as incense, lamps, water, food and flowers.

### Humanism
As Humanists do not believe in a god they do not have any form of worship.

### Islam
Muslims worship in a mosque (*masjid*). They also pray five times a day at home or at work. The mosque is a place to pray but also a community centre.

### Jainism
Worship in Jainism is about personal spiritual development rather than devotion or respect for a God. Jains worship in many ways. Some will go to temples to perform rituals and ceremonies in respect of the Tirthankaras. Others will worship at home.

### Judaism
Worship is important in Judaism and until the first century CE the Temple in Jerusalem was the main focus for worship. After the Temple was destroyed in CE 70 by Roman invaders, the synagogue grew in importance.

### Sikhism
Sikhs believe that worship is important and prayer and concentration on God is a feature of their worship. The Sikh place of worship is called a *gurdwara* which literally means 'the door to the *guru*'.

### Zoroastrianism
At first, Zoroastrians met together to worship on hilltops and mountainsides, gathered around a fire. Later, temples were built that housed a fire, known as 'fire temples'. Today many followers worship at home.

# Drawing it all together

## Learning about religion

1 Describe the place of worship and the way in which people worship in two of the religions you have studied.

2 Write a definition of these words:

   **sermon**

   **service.**

## Learning from religion

1 For two of the religions you have studied find out about private and public worship. Explain which you think is most important to believers and say why.

**Hint** In your explanation you could give your own opinion on the value for believers of the different forms of worship.

2 Choose two of the religions you have studied. Working with a partner, design a building which they can both use for worship.

**Hint** You need to think carefully about how followers of the two religions worship and what they need from a building to enable them to do this.

3 'It is worship which is important, not where it takes place.' Discuss this with a partner.

**Hint** Remember that you need to weigh up both sides of the argument.

# 2.5 How do people celebrate?

## What is a 'celebration'?

A **celebration** is a joyful occasion when a special event is marked or remembered. Within religions, there are many occasions when celebrations take place. Religious believers celebrate through their services of worship, in festivals or through important occasions such as births and marriages. These occasions bring people together to mark significant events.

Celebration has a central role within Christianity. Services highlight Christian beliefs and Christians celebrate through music, singing and prayer. The Christian year is organised around a series of festivals that celebrate Jesus' life, death and resurrection. They can also mark important events in the history of Christianity.

The Christian Year. How many Christian festivals do you recognise?

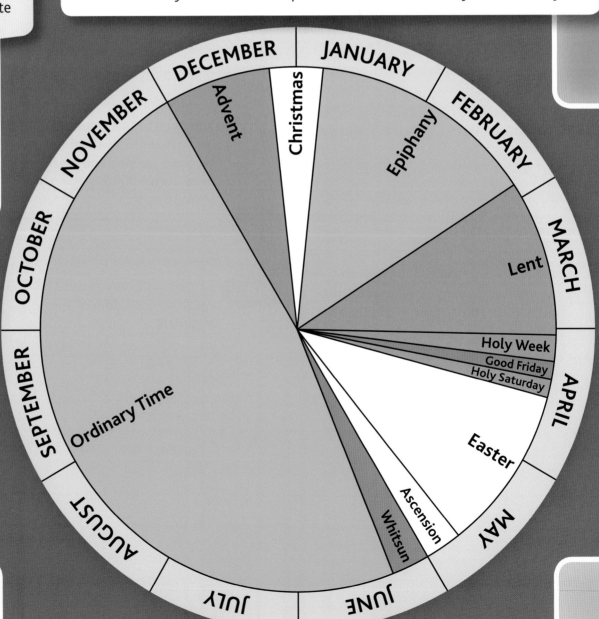

## Learning about religion

1 Choose a Christian festival and create a poster showing how Christians celebrate it.

2 Why do Christians think it is important to celebrate? Give three reasons.

# How do Christians celebrate festivals?

The best-known Christian festivals are Christmas, which celebrates the birth of Jesus, and Easter, which marks his death and resurrection. These festivals have gained non-religious importance and in many countries are national holidays. Many of these traditions are cultural rather than specifically religious.

### Christmas

- Christmas is celebrated in December and remembers the birth of Jesus Christ

- Advent calendars and candles are used in preparation for Christmas

- Families and friends share in this festival, often choosing to spend Christmas Day together

- Christians attend special church services – Midnight Mass takes place on Christmas Eve and many Christians attend a service on Christmas Day

- Carols are sung

- Cards and presents are given, just as Jesus received gifts from the *magi*

- Special food is eaten and shared

- Houses are decorated

- Nativity plays are performed, retelling the story of the birth of Jesus

### Holy Week and Easter

- The date of Easter is not fixed in the normal calendar; it changes each year

- Easter follows the 40-day season of Lent when Christians prepare themselves for Easter and remember Jesus' 40 days in the wilderness

- Church services remember the sacrifice Jesus made by dying on the cross

- Hot-cross buns are a special food traditionally eaten on Good Friday (the day of Jesus' crucifixion)

- Re-enactments of Jesus' death and resurrection (Passion plays) are staged

- Easter cards and eggs are given – the hollow egg symbolises the empty tomb of Jesus; the egg also symbolises the birth of new life and the resurrection of Jesus

# 2.5 How do people celebrate?

### Bahá'í
The Bahá'ís have created a new calendar which begins on 21 March, at the spring equinox. Many of their festivals remember important events in the lives of the Báb and Bahá'u'lláh.

### Hinduism
Hinduism has many festivals, most often celebrating nature's seasons, family relationships and special events in the lives of a saint or a god or goddess.

### Islam
In Islam, celebration is important and is often seen to be a way of thanking Allah. The family is at the centre of the Islamic faith so celebration usually involves the extended family unit.

### Judaism
Jewish celebrations can be about miracles that happened, festivals or to celebrate life cycle events.

### Zoroastrianism
Zoroastrians have many festivals, feast days and celebrations for initiations and weddings throughout the year. Many festivals are linked to the seasons. Celebrating the life of Zoroaster is also very important.

### Buddhism
In Buddhism many of the celebrations are related to the Buddha or important figures who are believed to have achieved enlightenment.

### Humanism
Humanists enjoy special holidays such as Christmas in secular ways, celebrating with their friends and families with presents and parties. Births, namings, marriages and partnerships are also celebrated.

### Jainism
Jain festivals have great importance. Festivals provide an opportunity for Jains to worship together and they are often a time when communities come together. Some Jain festivals celebrate an aspect from the lives of the Tirthankaras.

### Sikhism
Guru Amar Das Ji started a tradition of adapting Hindu festivals to Sikh ideas. These festivals today are known as *melas* or fairs. Some of the most important Sikh festivals are the *gurpurbs* which celebrate the lives of the *gurus*.

# Drawing it all together

## Learning about religion

1  Make two lists showing the different ways in which people celebrate in two of the religions you have studied.

2  Write a paragraph using the following terms and show that you understand them:

   anniversary
   festival.

## Learning from religion

1  What do you think are the most important ways in which people celebrate festivals or special days?

   **Hint** Remember to think about the reason for and purpose of the celebration.

2  You are going to create a new festival or day to celebrate. Explain what the day is called, what it celebrates and how the celebration will be done.

   **Hint** You need to think carefully about the reason for the celebration and show how this is shown in the way the day is celebrated.

3  'Most festivals are about things which happened in the past and are out of date now.' Discuss this with a partner.

   **Hint** Remember that some of the events which people celebrate are about key events in their religion.

# 2.6 Pilgrimage

## What is a pilgrimage?

A **pilgrimage** is a journey to a special place. In religion, it is a journey made by believers to a place that is holy or **sacred**. It may be a place where an important event happened, or one related to an important person, or simply somewhere that is considered holy.

These places are given great value by some religious believers and faith is often strengthened by followers making the effort to visit them. While a believer is on pilgrimage, they may choose to join in activities with other people to share the experience or they may prefer to spend time alone in prayer and reflection.

## Your lesson objectives

**In this lesson you will:**

- understand the term 'pilgrimage'
- investigate why Christians go on pilgrimage
- explore why some places are important to Christians.

**Can you identify which Christian place of pilgrimage this is? Describe what you can see. (Answer below.)**

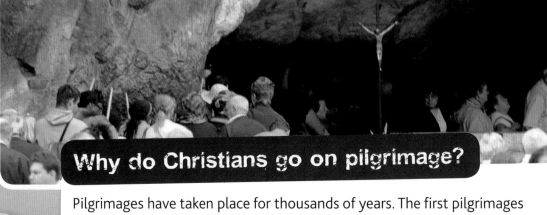

## Why do Christians go on pilgrimage?

Pilgrimages have taken place for thousands of years. The first pilgrimages would have been long, difficult and dangerous. For Christians, pilgrimage is an important part of their spiritual life. A pilgrimage is seen as a physical sign representing their faith.

Christians go on pilgrimage for many reasons:

- to trace the history of their religion or visit places where religious events occurred
- to get closer to God and feel connected to him spiritually
- to ask for forgiveness
- to ask for help if they are in need
- to be healed.

## Your key words

**pilgrimage**
a journey to a special place

**Pope**
the Bishop of Rome who is the leader of the Roman Catholic Church

**sacred**
considered to be special and holy

Pilgrims visit the grotto where the Virgin Mary is said to have appeared in Lourdes, France.

# Where do Christians go on pilgrimage?

### Bethlehem
The place where Jesus was born; a church has been built on the site. Pilgrims often offer prayers of thanks and sense a feeling of amazement that this is where Christianity began.

### Jerusalem
This holds particular significance for Christians as Jesus was crucified here. Some pilgrims follow the route Jesus took to his death. This is especially remembered during the festival of Easter.

### Rome
Rome has been central to the development of Christianity and today has particular importance for Roman Catholics as it is the home of the **Pope**. Pilgrims visit many well known places, including St Peter's Basilica and places with links to St Paul.

### Lourdes
Lourdes attracts millions of pilgrims every year. Its importance is linked to a vision of the Virgin Mary that was seen there by a young French girl, and there has been evidence of healing miracles taking place in Lourdes. Many sick people go in the hope of being cured.

## Learning about religion

1 Explain your understanding of the term 'pilgrimage'.

2 Why do you think pilgrimage is important to Christians? Use examples to illustrate your answer.

3 Look at the reasons why Christians go on pilgrimage. Can you think of any others? Rank them in order of importance.

4 Write two sentences about each Christian place of pilgrimage.

# 2.6 Pilgrimage

### Bahá'í
Bahá'ís may apply to undertake a pilgrimage. This lasts nine days and consists of guided visits to the holy shrines and other sites in the Holy Land associated with the central figures of the faith.

### Buddhism
Pilgrimage is important in Buddhism as the Buddha spoke about pilgrimage helping spiritual development. There are key places identified for pilgrimage in Buddhism including places that relate directly to the life of the Buddha.

### Hinduism
Hindus consider India a land of spiritual significance. The many pilgrimage sites include cities, temples, roadside shrines, holy rivers, sacred mountains and other spots historically linked to saints and avatars (incarnations of God).

### Humanism
As they do not believe in a god, Humanists do not make pilgrimages to particular places.

### Jainism
Jainism teaches that pilgrimage is important. There are many places within India that have special importance in Jainism because they are associated with events of the past.

### Islam
Pilgrimage in Islam is a duty. *Hajj* or pilgrimage to Makkah is one of the Five Pillars. Muslims are expected to try and complete *Hajj* once in their lifetime.

### Judaism
Since the destruction of the Temple in Jerusalem by Roman invaders in CE 70, Jews have not brought offerings to the Temple. However, Jerusalem has become a key place for Jews to visit.

### Sikhism
Pilgrimage is not a requirement in Sikhism. Sikhs do not believe that the action of pilgrimage necessarily helps them to develop spiritually. The real pilgrimage that counts in the life of a Sikh is the journey within to seek a union with God.

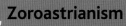
### Zoroastrianism
As Islam spread throughout Iran, many Zoroastrian fire temples were abandoned. However, they are still seen as sacred places and many Zoroastrians undertake pilgrimages to visit these sites, as well as the many other fire temples in Iran and India.

# Drawing it all together

## Learning about religion

1 Write a short paragraph on the different ways in which people may make a pilgrimage in two of the religions you have studied.

2 Write a definition of these words:

healing

miracle.

## Learning from religion

1 What are the most important reasons for going on a pilgrimage?

**Hint** Remember to give your own opinion as well as different religious reasons.

2 If you were going on a pilgrimage where would you go and why?

**Hint** You need to think carefully about the reason for making this pilgrimage. It may be to a place you have always wanted to see, perhaps a country, a sports arena or something associated with a religion.

3 Discuss with a partner what you think the following statement means. 'The whole of life is a pilgrimage so there is no need to go to special places.'

**Hint** Try to give reasons for your opinions.

# 2.7 Why celebrate?

## Your lesson objectives

**In this lesson you will:**

- explore reasons why people celebrate
- consider the role of celebration in the lives of Christians.

## Why do people celebrate?

Celebration is about bringing people together and sharing beliefs at special times. Events such as birthdays, anniversaries and passing exams are occasions to share; people want friends and family to join them in celebrating at these times.

Celebrations can also be about remembering and learning from the past. The death of a loved one is a sad time, but it is a chance to celebrate their life and recognise their achievements. Tragedies in the world are often marked in some way, not because they are joyful occasions, but to remember what happened and to share the hope that it will not happen again.

## Why do Christians celebrate important events?

Celebration has a long history within Christianity. The Christian year is based around a series of festivals that celebrate major events, mainly connected to the life of Jesus. Having a set cycle of festivals means that Christians can look forward to these events and experience shared beliefs. Christians believe that celebration helps to strengthen their identity and unite them as a community. They also feel it is important to remember and celebrate past events in their religion. Festival celebrations remind Christians of past events and the beliefs they hold today.

The festival of Christmas is important in remembering the birth of Jesus Christ. It is a time for family and to think of others. Similarly, Easter is an important festival. It marks the events leading up to the death and resurrection of Jesus. His resurrection is particularly important as it gives Christians hope of life after death.

## Celebration through worship

Celebration through worship is important. It allows the Christian community to share their love for God and praise him. It is also an opportunity to ask for help or comfort in times of need. Christians attending church regularly develop their relationship with God and mix with other believers who share the same beliefs.

A procession for lighting the New Fire on Holy Saturday in the Ancash province of Peru.

## Learning about religion

1   Make a list of the reasons why people celebrate.

2   How important do you think celebration is in Christianity? Give three reasons for your answer.

3   Why do Christians celebrate the festivals of Christmas and Easter?

# 2.7 Why celebrate?

### Bahá'í
Like many religions the Bahá'í Faith celebrates festivals associated with God. Each month recalls one of the attributes of God. The last month of the calendar is celebrated with a 19-day Fast, which is a time for gift-giving and charitable works.

### Buddhism
Devotion in Buddhism involves showing respect to the Buddha and the celebration of festivals has a role in achieving this. They are a time when the Buddhist community can come together and share in their beliefs.

### Hinduism
Hindu festivals bring together families and communities. They help Hindus put aside their worldly concerns to focus the mind on the real self, the Supreme and spiritual practice.

### Humanism
Although there are no compulsory rituals or celebrations for Humanists there are secular ceremonies for weddings, baby-namings and funerals.

### Islam
Celebrations in Islam are seen as an opportunity to give thanks to Allah for his blessings and kindness. Festivals in Islam involve worship and care for others. Muslims share with family and friends, but also with the poor.

### Jainism
Much of Jain worship is done alone so festivals provide an opportunity for Jains to worship together and they are often a time when communities come together. Many Jain festivals celebrate an aspect of the lives of the Tirthankaras.

### Judaism
In Judaism there is a major or minor festival celebrated in almost every month of the year. Most celebrations remember events in Jewish history and unite the Jewish community.

### Sikhism
Festivals in Sikhism are an important opportunity for Sikhs to rededicate themselves to their faith and reaffirm their beliefs. They are celebrated to inspire the faithful followers and remind them of their history and where the beliefs and teachings began.

### Zoroastrianism
Zoroastrians have many festivals that take place in the year but they also celebrate important events in people's lives. The most important of these is known as the Navjote ceremony of initiation into the religion and the community.

# Drawing it all together

## Learning about religion

1 For two or more of the religions you have studied list the different reasons why people celebrate.

2 Write a paragraph using the following terms and show that you understand them:

> resurrection
>
> tradition.

## Learning from religion

1 What do you think are the most important reasons for celebrating?

**Hint** In your answer you should refer to non-religious celebrations as well as religious ones.

2 One of the most important parts of celebrating religious festivals is that people come together as a community. Explain how you think this might help people in their lives.

**Hint** Remember to think about all the different ways in which people might be affected.

3 'Having celebrations is one of the most important parts of a religion.' Discuss this with a partner and compare your ideas.

**Hint** You need to think about all the other parts of religious life as well as celebrations, to decide what you feel is most important.

# 2.8 How do people experience God?

## What does it mean to experience God?

God is at the centre of Christianity and it is towards God that Christian worship is directed. **Revelation** is the experience of God showing himself to believers. Many Christians feel they experience God in some way, which can take many different forms: visible or invisible; physical or spiritual. Christians often talk of experiencing the power of God. This is God acting in the world, either through humans or through the Holy Spirit. Throughout history there have been many reports of Christians experiencing God.

### worship

Worshipping regularly offers Christians time to praise God and deepen their relationship with him. It allows them to reflect on beliefs and experience God in their lives.

### visions

There have been many reported visions in Christianity, such as the Virgin Mary appearing at Lourdes, now a Christian place of pilgrimage. Experiencing a vision associated with God confirms faith and reassures Christians that God is watching over them.

## Learning about religion

1 Create a poster showing some of the ways in which Christians believe God can be experienced. Use images as well as words.

2 Which ways of experiencing God do you think would be the most powerful? Give three reasons for your answer.

## prayer

Prayer is a form of communication with God. It is a way of reflecting on God, asking him for help or thanking him. Christians believe God hears their prayers and answers them.

## miracles

A miracle is something amazing that would not normally happen but Christians believe it is God working within the world.

**Your discussion**

Do you have to experience God in order to believe in God?

## reading sacred texts

The Bible has a special meaning for Christians. It is considered to be the Word of God and many Christians feel inspired reading it as they feel God is speaking directly to them.

## How do Christians experience God?

## the natural world

Christians believe God is the creator of the world and one way of experiencing him is to study his creation. There are many beautiful things in nature and Christians may feel awe and wonder looking at them.

## life after death

Christians believe death is not the end and they will be united with God in Heaven. This is the ultimate experience of God.

## inner, personal feeling

Many Christians feel God is present supporting them, even when things are going wrong in their lives. They believe they have a personal connection with God and that he is watching over them.

## inspirational Christians

These are people who have received an experience from God and they inspire others to follow their example and do God's work in the world.

# 2.8 How do people experience God?

### Bahá'í
The Bahá'í Faith teaches that God is beyond human understanding but people can learn what God is like and come closer to him through prayer, meditation, fasting and charitable deeds.

### Hinduism
Hindus believe the real self and God can be experienced in two main ways: first, through *puja* (ritual worship of the sacred image) and, secondly, though *yoga* (union with God) and meditation.

### Jainism
Jains believe that by praising and worshipping the Tirthankaras and following the path that they established, they too will experience their own souls.

### Sikhism
Sikhs believe that worship allows them to experience God. In worship, they sing hymns and recite prayers to praise God. Devoting their lives to helping others pleases God according to Sikhs, which is a way of experiencing him.

### Buddhism
Buddhists do not believe in a supreme god and so they do not think that they can experience him or her.

### Humanism
As Humanists do not believe in a god they do not have any belief in religious experience.

### Islam
Muslims believe in One God, Allah. Muslims hold many beliefs about Allah including the idea that although Muslims cannot fully understand him they can experience him in their lives.

### Judaism
Jews can experience and get closer to G-d in many different ways. Jews accept that the Torah is G-d's word and believe that study of this will help them understand what G-d wants them to do.

### Zoroastrianism
Zoroastrians believe that Ahura Mazda (God) is beyond human understanding. Ahura Mazda created the world, he is not a part of creation. He was not created and he is timeless. However, he can be experienced in the world, especially before the sacred fire.

# Drawing it all together

## Learning about religion

1 For two or more of the religions you have studied list the different ways in which people believe they can experience God.

2 Write a definition of these words:

**experience**
**physical**
**prayer**
**spiritual.**

## Learning from religion

1 What do you think people mean when they say they have had a spiritual experience? How do you think this might affect them?

**Hint** Remember that people have different types of religious experience.

2 Working in pairs, prepare a short presentation for the class to describe what you think it would be like to have a religious experience.

**Hint** You should base your presentation on what you have learnt about religious experiences from the religions you have studied.

3 'The only real way to experience God is to talk to him when you pray.' Discuss this with a partner and compare your ideas.

**Hint** Think about all the other ways in which people say they experience God.

# 2.9 How can belief affect someone's daily life?

## Your lesson objectives

**In this lesson you will:**

- explain the relationship between belief and action
- explore the importance of religious faith in the lives of Christians
- consider some of the difficulties for Christians of living by their faith.

## What is the relationship between belief and action?

There is a strong link between belief and action. Many religious believers claim that religious belief and faith are meaningless if they do not apply them in their lives. Indeed, many people would argue that it is wrong to believe something and act differently. Holding certain beliefs affects the lives of religious believers. For example, if they believe all human life is special and a gift from God, they should, in their actions, try to help other humans however they can, such as through charity work or helping the homeless.

Stone tablet in the USA showing the Ten Commandments. How easy is it for Christians to apply the Ten Commandments to their everyday lives?

## Your key words

**forgiveness**

no longer feeling anger or resentment towards someone who has caused you suffering

**multicultural**

made up of people from many different cultures

**secular**

having no spiritual or religious basis

## How do Christian beliefs affect the life of a Christian?

Christians look to the Bible for guidance on how to live. They believe that rules such as the Ten Commandments and Jesus' teachings tell them how they should behave and what is acceptable. Christians believe they should not lie, steal or murder, as these things are forbidden by the Ten Commandments. Christian beliefs about God suggest that they need to develop a personal relationship with God, and therefore Christians may pray every day and attend worship regularly. Christians also try to follow the Golden Rule which Jesus taught: 'Do to others as you would have them do to you' (Luke 6:31). They also feel that there are ideas they should apply in their lives, such as appreciating the world because it is God's creation and helping other people, as that is what God wants. They believe that God instructs them to consider how their actions affect others and to apply Christian ideas such as **forgiveness**. Christian beliefs are not selected at random – they are rules and guidance to be applied every day in order for Christians to live as God intended.

# GOD'S TEN COMMANDMENTS

THE LORD YOUR GOD
BROUGHT YOU OUT
HE LAND OF EGYPT,
PLACE OF SLAVERY.
U SHALL HAVE NO
R GODS BESIDES ME.

SHALL NOT TAKE
NAME OF THE LORD
AIN. FOR THE LORD
NOT HOLD HIM

IV  HONOR YOUR FATHER AND
YOUR MOTHER, THAT YOUR
DAYS MAY BE LONG IN THE
LAND WHICH THE LORD
YOUR GOD GIVES YOU

V  YOU SHALL NOT

VI  YOU SHALL
COMMIT ADULTERY

VII  YOU SHALL NOT STEAL

VIII  YOU

## How difficult is it to be a Christian today?

Today's society is **multicultural** and, some would argue, **secular**. This means that living as a Christian is more challenging. Life moves at a faster pace and people are surrounded by material goods. For many people, Sunday is no longer kept as a day of rest. This is not to say it is impossible to live as a Christian, just that there are new and different challenges. Part of being a Christian is learning to overcome challenges to the faith to show more commitment to the religion.

## Learning about religion

1  Explain in your own words the relationship between the ideas of belief and action.

2  Explain how Christian beliefs may affect the life of a Christian.

3  Draw up two lists. In one, list all the benefits of being a Christian today and in the other, list the challenges a Christian may face.

# 2.9 How can belief affect someone's daily life?

### Bahá'í
Bahá'ís must show their belief in ordinary daily life. They believe work done in the spirit of service to humanity is as important to God as prayer and worship, and performing useful work is considered a form of worship.

### Hinduism
The Hindu world view and its associated values influence the way followers see and respond to life. For example, they see the presence of a soul in all life forms and therefore have compassion. This means that many Hindus refuse to eat meat or to be otherwise involved in killing.

### Islam
Islam is a religion that believes submission to God is essential. For Muslims, this involves a conscious commitment to a life of thankfulness and obedience to God, which includes all their actions.

### Judaism
Religion is seen to affect every aspect of Jewish life – food, what is worn, how Jews spend their time. For a Jew, their beliefs and actions are strongly linked, as they obey G-d's commandments.

### Buddhism
Because of their beliefs, Buddhists think it is important to try and address the suffering that is in the world. They also believe in non-violence and in trying to help others in society.

### Humanism
Humanists believe that this is the only life we have. They think that they must create their own meaning and purpose and should try to live a full and happy life and help other people to do the same.

### Jainism
Jainism is strongly focused on the soul and the aim of a Jain is to try and achieve liberation for their soul from the constant cycle of rebirth. The link between beliefs and actions is very important as they want to perform good actions in order to achieve their goal. They should show awareness in all their actions, be vegetarian and show compassion towards all lives.

### Sikhism
For Sikhs, a good life is one which is in tune with God so their beliefs are directly related to their actions in everyday life.

### Zoroastrianism
Zoroastrians promise to try to live lives of good thoughts, good words and good deeds (actions). This has an effect on how they live their lives every day, for example praying will help them to have good thoughts.

# Drawing it all together

## Learning about religion

**1** For two or more of the religions you have studied write a short paragraph about the different ways in which belief affects the life of a believer.

**2** Write a paragraph using the following terms and show that you understand them:

   **creation**

   **forgiveness.**

## Learning from religion

**1** Discuss with a partner how the different beliefs which are found in a multicultural society might be shown in how people live.

**Hint** In your answer you need to look at different religions as well as the different effects of belief.

**2** Think about a way in which what you believe has affected what you do. Write a passage explaining this.

**Hint** Remember that in your answer you do not necessarily have to write about a religious belief.

**3** 'People can live good lives without needing to believe in a god.' Discuss this with a partner and compare your ideas.

**Hint** First, consider what you think is a 'good life'.

# Your Assessment

Make a list of different forms of worship you have learnt about in this chapter.

Then write an article for a school magazine explaining the value of one of these from the point of view of a believer.

**Hint** Remember to look at different religions as well as different types of worship.

# 3 Beliefs about God and the meaning of life

## The bigger picture

Have you ever wondered where the world came from? Have you ever asked yourself what the purpose of you being on earth is – what is the meaning of life? In this chapter you will consider some of the questions that have been puzzling philosophers for thousands of years.

You will consider questions about God and the world around us, as well as what happens after death and why humans consider themselves to be unique.

You will be asked to reflect on your own beliefs as well as learn what different religions believe about these issues.

It will be a journey of mystery and intrigue and by the end you should have a better understanding of why there are still many unanswered questions in the world.

### Learning about religion

1 Why do you think people are so puzzled about questions which deal with God and the world around us?

2 Religious people always seem to be concerned about what might happen to people after they die. Why do you think this?

### Your discussion

'We will never be able to offer an answer to the question, "What is the meaning of life?"'
Discuss this claim.

# 3 Introduction
# What are 'ultimate questions'?

**Who is God?**

**Where did the world come from?**

**Are prayers answered?**

**What is the meaning of life?**

## Your lesson objectives

**In this lesson you will:**

- explore what ultimate questions are

- reflect on how ultimate questions can be answered

- consider your own thoughts about ultimate questions.

Ultimate questions are the 'big' questions in life that seem to have no single definite answer. They are questions concerning the meaning of life, the purpose of humans and the issues that arise when talking about God. Ultimate questions are not easy to answer, because science and logic do not provide the **evidence** required to give **proof** of the answers. Ultimate questions have been around since the first human beings, and have puzzled many people who have tried to answer them.

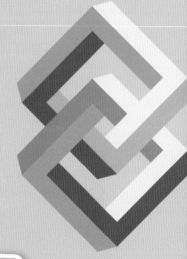

**Who am I?**

**What is 'the soul'?**

**What happens when we die?**

The following quotations are all about the ultimate question 'What is the meaning of life?' Think about what each of them is trying to say.

The purpose of life is a life of purpose.
(Robert Byrne 1928– )

We make a living by what we get, we make a life by what we give.
(Winston Churchill 1874–1975)

Learn from yesterday, live for today, hope for tomorrow.
(Anonymous)

Life is like a box of chocolates.
(From the film *Forrest Gump*, 1994)

## Can ultimate questions be answered?

It is human nature to want to understand the world. Humans actively seek knowledge, and this is something that people often claim makes them different from all other forms of creation. Philosophers have tried to offer answers for thousands of years, and these answers have changed as knowledge has been gained and some questions have been answered by science. However, science has not been able to answer all the questions that puzzle humans.

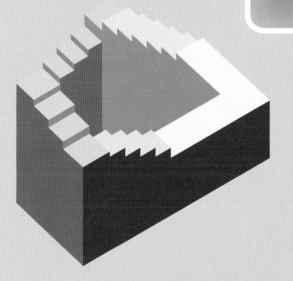

## Learning about religion

1 Write down five ultimate questions of your own.

2 With a partner:

   a  Try to answer the questions you created for question 1.

   b  Could you answer them? Why, or why not?

   c  Where might you look to try to answer them?

3 Why do you think ultimate questions cause so many problems?

4 How do Christians attempt to answer ultimate questions?

There are many ways of looking at these images but can we tell which is right?

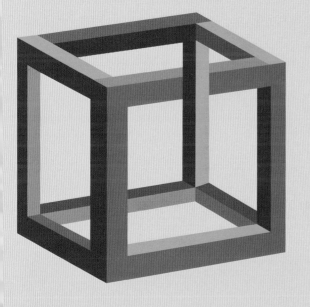

## Your key words

**belief**
accepting that something is true or real

**evidence**
facts that can be used as proof

**faith**
belief in somebody or something especially without logical proof

**proof**
evidence that something is true or exists

**soul**
the spiritual part of a human regarded as immortal

Christians would argue that there may be many explanations for ultimate questions and that mysteries are part of their **faith**. Christian **beliefs** help Christians to make sense of the world and answer questions that seem difficult. They have offered answers to questions such as 'Where did the world come from?' and 'Why is there evil and suffering in the world?' The responses, however, still do not offer proof. They are based on faith, which means putting your trust in something. Christians argue that their faith helps them understand the world, and there will always be questions that we cannot answer, just as God is an idea that humans will never fully understand.

# 3 Introduction
# What are 'ultimate questions'?

### Bahá'í
Bahá'ís accept the truth of most of the world's religions. They believe that as God reveals more through the central figures of these faiths so humans come to a better understanding of ultimate questions.

### Buddhism
Buddhism is based on the teachings of the Buddha (*Dhamma/Dharma*). Buddhists believe that through the teachings of the Buddha, they will see and understand things as they truly are.

### Hinduism
Hinduism teaches that asking ultimate questions, especially of the *guru* (spiritual teacher), is crucial to a person's spiritual progress. Philosophical insight helps the seeker to strengthen their religious beliefs and achieve liberation.

### Humanism
Humanists believe that there is no ultimate 'meaning' of life but that humans should make their own meaning.

### Islam
Islam is a religion based on faith and trust. Muslims believe that what Islam teaches is true and it provides answers to all of the difficult questions in life in some way.

### Jainism
Jainism attempts to answer ultimate questions through its teachings and following the example of the Tirthankaras. Jains do not accept the traditional view of a god, therefore their understanding of the world automatically addresses some of the ultimate questions.

### Judaism
Judaism provides rules and guidelines for a Jew to follow. It also provides answers to many ultimate questions. The Torah addresses many of the issues involved, describing the purpose of life as being to obey G-d and worship him.

### Sikhism
There are many ultimate questions which Sikhs believe their faith addresses. Sikhs spend their lives on a journey of learning. Therefore, answers to ultimate questions are something they see as discovering for themselves.

### Zoroastrianism
The prophet Zoroaster was able to give answers to many of the ultimate questions people asked about the world around them. He had spent his life asking questions and was given the answers in the form of visions of God.

# Drawing it all together

## Learning about religion

**1** For two or more of the religions you have studied explain how followers believe they can find the answers to 'ultimate questions'.

**2** Write a definition of these words:

logic

science

ultimate questions.

## Learning from religion

**1** What do you think are the six most important 'ultimate questions'?

**Hint** You may find that some of your questions are different from the ones usually thought of in religions.

**2** Think about any way in which an ultimate question has affected what you believe or think. Write a paragraph explaining this.

**Hint** Remember that in your answer you do not necessarily have to write about a religious belief.

**3** 'Ultimate questions can be answered by people themselves and there is no need for religion to explain them.' Discuss this with a partner and compare your ideas.

**Hint** Remember to consider different questions and different responses.

# 3.1 How do we know if God exists?

## Your lesson objectives

**In this lesson you will:**

- explore the terms 'theist', 'atheist' and 'agnostic'

- understand some of the arguments for and against the existence of God.

## Your key words

**agnostic**

someone who believes that some things cannot be fully known

**atheist**

someone who believes there is no god

**Bible**

a word used for the sacred writings of the Jews (Tenakh) and Christians (Old and New Testaments)

**complex**

made up of many parts; complicated

**theist**

someone who believes there is a God

**worship**

to show love, respect or devotion to someone or something

## Belief in God

'God' is a difficult idea to understand. The question 'How do you know if God exists?' is challenging, mainly because people today tend to rely on scientific evidence and there is none that proves his existence. Perhaps the question we should be asking is 'Do we need to prove the existence of God?' Religious believers such as Christians put their faith in God's existence and accept that, even though they may not be able to 'see' God, there are other ways of experiencing him and knowing God exists.

There are some people who believe in the existence of God, others who believe there is no God and some who are unsure about the existence of God. There are special terms used for these: **theist**, **atheist** and **agnostic**.

$$\frac{(P_0 - C_1) + P^2 (\sqrt{b}}{D + N_2 \left(\frac{B}{b_2}\right) + E}$$

## What arguments are there against the existence of God?

Many people believe that there is no god. This may be because of their upbringing or because they do not know about or understand religious views. It may also be because they have decided that they do not need to have belief in a god in order to lead happy and fulfilling lives. Sometimes, bad experiences are taken as evidence of there being no God. Terrible tragedies happen every day and many people argue that a truly loving God would not let people suffer.

Science uses evidence such as mathematical equations to prove ideas.

= God?

## What arguments support God's existence?

Many Christians point towards the evidence of religious experience, when someone has a vision or perhaps experiences a miracle, which they attribute to God. They believe God can be known through the **Bible** and **worship**. Christians also argue that religion is having faith in things you cannot see and Christian teachings tell them God is real.

There are several more arguments for God's existence.

### Cosmological Argument

Everything has a cause and for anything to exist there must have been a First Cause. The universe was created by a First Cause and that cause is assumed to be God.

### Ontological Argument

God exists because people cannot think of anything greater than God.

### Teleological Argument

Everything in nature shows order, purpose and beauty and is **complex**. Just as if you looked into a wind-up watch you would assume that it had been created by a watchmaker, so anything as complex as the world must have had a creator and that creator must have been God.

### Pascal's Wager

Blaise Pascal (1623–62) wrote that even though it was not possible to prove that God exists, people might as well believe in God because they had nothing to lose and possibly everything to gain.

## Learning about religion

1  Copy the definitions of a theist, an atheist and an agnostic. Try to write at least two reasons for each view underneath.

2  Summarise what you think a Christian might say in response to the question 'How do you know God exists?'

3  Do you think it will ever be possible to prove or disprove the existence of God?
    Why, or why not?

## Why are some people agnostics?

Some people believe that it is not possible to know whether God exists or not. They are not prepared to say he does not exist, but equally they do not want to say that he definitely does. They believe that ultimate questions such as 'Does God exist?' are important but unanswerable.

# 3.1 How do we know if God exists?

## Bahá'í
Bahá'ís believe that a series of God's messengers have brought teachings at various times in history. Bahá'u'lláh is believed by Bahá'ís to be the most recent of these but not the final one.

## Buddhism
Buddhism has been described as a 'non-theistic' religion because Buddhists do not believe in a supreme god. Many Buddhists would consider themselves to be agnostic as they do not believe god's existence can be known.

## Hinduism
Hinduism tries to investigate the nature of the self, which most Hindus consider to be part of the eternal spirit or Supreme (Brahman). Hinduism is seen as believing both in one God, Brahman, and in many other gods through whom Brahman is worshipped.

## Humanism
Humanism is based on reason, not on faith. Humanists believe that science gives the best explanations for the existence of the universe and life on earth. They do not accept that there is any evidence that the universe was created by a god or gods.

## Islam
God is at the centre of Islamic faith. Muslims believe there is One God, Allah, and this belief is contained in the 'Declaration of Faith', the Shahadah.

## Jainism
Jainism does not accept a creator god. Jains believe that everything that exists in the world today was never created and will never be destroyed.

## Judaism
Judaism is a monotheistic religion, accepting belief in one G-d. Jews believe that G-d was revealed through the Torah and revelations to the prophets. They do not believe it is possible to understand G-d fully but they understand the teachings that were revealed.

## Sikhism
The fundamental belief in Sikhism is that God exists. The Guru Granth Sahib Ji begins with the phrase '*Ik Onkar*' meaning 'One God'. It is accepted that God does not just exist as an idea but as a real being which cannot be described.

## Zoroastrianism
Zoroastrians believe in one supreme God, Ahura Mazda, who appeared to the prophet Zoroaster, founder of the religion.

# Drawing it all together

## Learning about religion

1 For two or more of the religions you have studied write a short paragraph on the reasons believers give when they say that they know God exists.

2 Write a paragraph using the following terms and show that you understand them:

  **evidence**

  **vision.**

## Learning from religion

1 Make two lists. In one give reasons to believe that God exists, in the other give reasons to think that God does not exist.

**Hint** You should give religious and non-religious reasons.

2 Working with a partner create a presentation explaining what you think God might be like.

**Hint** You should include in your answer religious beliefs as well as your own views.

3 'If God does not answer people's prayers then he cannot exist.' Discuss this with a partner and compare your ideas.

**Hint** Try to consider all the different opinions there might be about this statement.

# 3.2 Images of God

## How can we describe God?

There are many words we may think of when considering God. Young children may imagine God as an old man with a white beard, perhaps floating on a cloud. As they grow up and their ideas change, many people do not know how to put an image to God, as God is not something human and therefore understandable. Modern representations of God have shown him as having no real form. God is represented as a mass of flowing shapes and colours to show he is like a spirit, rather than a human. Christians would say that the ultimate image of God is as a human being in Jesus Christ.

### Your lesson objectives

**In this lesson you will:**

- explore how images help Christians to understand ideas about God

- investigate the importance of images in describing God.

This is a representation of God, painted by Michelangelo. The painting is called *The Creation of the Sun and Moon* and is found in the Sistine Chapel, Vatican City, Italy. Why do you think the artist has shown God like this?

### Your key words

**symbol**

an action, image, object or picture that is used to represent something else

## Is God a man?

In Christianity, God is traditionally referred to as being male. The Bible also generally takes this view and words such as 'Father', 'Lord' and 'King' are used. Does this mean that God is male? Most Christians would argue that God really cannot be understood as male or female, since these are human ideas and God is a spirit. Some Christians also use the word 'Mother' to refer to God, which can also be found in the Bible. They believe that this emphasises God's caring and nurturing nature, as a mother cares for her child.

## How do images help Christians understand ideas about God?

Images and **symbols** often represent ideas that are difficult to express in words. For Christians, using images to represent God helps to make God more personal, so that believers can relate to him more easily. It helps them to consider him in human terms rather than as something spiritual which they cannot grasp or understand. Symbols or images also remind Christians of aspects of their faith. For example, Christians believe that Jesus was God's son who died on a cross to save human beings from the results of their sins. By using the image of a cross to remind them of this, Christians are remembering that God loved his creation so much that he sent Jesus to earth as its saviour.

### Your discussion

'We should not have any images of God because we have no idea what God looks like.'

What is your view on this statement?

## Learning about religion

1 Write down ten words that you feel describe God. (They can describe God's character or what God looks like.)

2 Does the picture show what you think God is like? Why or why not?

3 Make a list of reasons why images of God help Christians.

4 Find three different images of God.

  a Write a description of each picture.
  b Say how the images are similar/ different.
  c Say which image you prefer and why.

# 3.2 Images of God

### Bahá'í
Bahá'ís believe that it would be wrong to try to make any images of God.

### Hinduism

Almost all Hindus believe in one God, either as a formless spirit or with a number of different forms showing individual richness and personality. The many images symbolically represent God's boundless forms, attributes and activities.

### Islam
Islam forbids any images of Allah. To make one would be thought of as committing *shirk* – considering something as being equal to Allah.

### Judaism
The second of the Ten Commandments forbids Jews from making images of 'what is in the heavens above, or on the earth below, or in the waters under the earth'. This also includes G-d.

### Zoroastrianism
Zoroastrians do not make images of Ahura Mazda because they believe that he has no body or physical existence.

### Buddhism
As Buddhists do not believe in a supreme creator god they do not create any images of a god.

### Humanism
Humanists do not believe in a god and so do not have images of one.

### Jainism

Jains do not believe in a traditional creator god but they do believe that there are 24 Tirthankaras who established the Jain path to liberation and who are worthy of worship in the same way as a god. They use representations of the Tirthankaras in their worship to help remind them of the path they took to liberation.

### Sikhism
Sikhs do not make images of God. Instead he is represented by symbols such as *Ik Onkar*. However, they do have pictures of the ten human *gurus*.

# Drawing it all together

## Learning about religion

1 Explain what two or more of the religions you have studied believe about making images of God. You might also include why, within some religions, people have different opinions about this.

2 Write a definition of these words:

   representation

   saviour.

## Learning from religion

1 Think about why images are useful. Write a paragraph explaining why sometimes images can tell people more than using words.

**Hint** You should try to use some religious as well as non-religious images.

2 Choose one religion which does have images of God. Find some images of this God and discuss with a partner what you can learn from these about the religion's beliefs.

**Hint** You should use as many different images as you can.

3 'Having images of God helps people when they are praying.' Discuss this with a partner and compare your ideas.

**Hint** Think about the ways in which images might both help and hinder prayer.

# 3.3 What do people believe about God?

## Your lesson objectives

**In this lesson you will:**

- learn what Christians believe about God
- understand the Christian idea of the Trinity
- understand why beliefs about God are important for Christians.

## Your key words

**doctrine**
teaching

**Heaven**
a place of paradise and reward in the presence of God

**Holy Spirit**
one person of the Trinity, the other two being the Father and the Son

**immanent**
the belief that God is within every human and so involved in the world

**monotheistic**
believing in one god

**transcendent**
beyond human understanding

**Trinity**
the mystery of one God in three persons: Father, Son and as Holy Spirit

## What do Christians believe about God?

Christianity is a **monotheistic** religion, which means that Christians believe there is only one God. They believe that God is the creator of the universe, as described in the Book of Genesis in the Bible. They use many different words for God such as 'Father' or 'Mother', 'Lord' and 'Almighty'.

It is very difficult to describe God in human terms, since Christians believe he is not human but spiritual. They believe he is **transcendent**, which means he is beyond human understanding, and yet at the same time they believe he is **immanent**, which means he is close to humans and involved in life on earth. Christians use the word 'holy' to describe God, as they believe he is perfect. They also refer to him as a judge, because they believe that after death he will judge them on their actions on earth.

## What is the Trinity?

Although God is believed to be one God, Christians understand who God is as three distinct persons. This is known as the **doctrine** of the **Trinity**, the idea that God is three persons: as Father, as Son and as **Holy Spirit.**

- God the FATHER means God is the creator of **Heaven** and earth. He is seen as being powerful, loving, eternal and all-knowing.

- God the SON is Jesus. God came to earth in human form to show people how they should live and died to pay for their sins. His resurrection gives Christians hope of life after death.

- God the HOLY SPIRIT is the presence of God. After the resurrection of Jesus, God sent the Holy Spirit to earth to guide and comfort people, so Christians know that God is always with them.

This altarpiece in Holy Trinity Church, Klenovnik, Varaždinska, Croatia shows the three persons of the Trinity.

## What does the Bible teach Christians about?

Beliefs about God are central to Christianity. The Bible explores the idea of God. Jesus provided a deeper understanding of the relationship between God and his creation by calling him 'Abba' – 'Daddy'. The Bible tells Christians what God is like and the Trinity helps them to understand God's different aspects. Christians strive to get closer to God. This may be by reading the Bible, by following the example of Jesus, through worship or by following the rules of Christianity.

## Learning about religion

1 Use the information on this page to make a list of some of the words Christians use to describe God and write a definition for each one.

2 What is the doctrine of the Trinity and how do Christians use it?

3 Create an ideas map summarising all the information you know about God in Christianity.

# 3.3 What do people believe about God?

## Bahá'í
In the Bahá'í Faith God is described as a single, eternal being who created all things, including all the creatures and forces in the universe. The existence of God is thought to be eternal, without a beginning or end.

## Hinduism
Hindus believe God dwells in three places: everywhere as an impersonal energy (Brahman), within the hearts of all creatures (Antaryami) and beyond this world as a person with unlimited goodness in every way (Bhagavan).

## Islam
Islam is a monotheistic religion, which means Muslims believe in One God, Allah. Belief in One God is known as *tawhid*.

## Judaism
Judaism is a monotheistic religion and the idea of there being one G-d is one of the most important beliefs. Jews believe G-d created the universe and holds it all together as he is involved in his creation.

## Buddhism
Buddhists do not believe in a supreme god. Buddhism may be referred to as a non-theistic religion as there is no recognition of a personal god to whom prayers can be directed. Siddhattha Gotama/Siddartha Goutama, the Buddha, is not thought of as a god.

## Humanism
Humanists do not believe in a god and rely instead on human reason and intellect.

## Jainism
Jainism does not recognise a god in the same way as other religions. Jains consider pure souls that have achieved liberation as god-like beings.

## Sikhism
The belief in one God is central to Sikhism. The *Ik Onkar* symbol, which means 'One God', is often on display in Sikh homes and *gurdwara*s to remind Sikhs of this belief.

## Zoroastrianism
The concept of God in Zoroastrianism is the earliest known example of a monotheistic religion, one that worships a single god. In the case of Zoroastrianism, this means believing in Ahura Mazda.

# Drawing it all together

## Learning about religion

**1** From two or more of the religions which you have studied explain what they believe about God and why these things are important.

**2** Write a paragraph using the following terms and show that you understand them:

> **creator**
>
> **universe**.

## Learning from religion

**1** Write a passage explaining what you believe about God. If you do not believe in God then explain why.

**Hint** Try to use some of the specialist words about God in this section and show that you understand them.

**2** Hinduism is a religion that has specific female gods. Discuss with a partner what difference it might make if people thought of God as a woman rather than a man.

**Hint** In your discussion be careful not to use stereotypes of men and women.

**3** 'The most important thing to believe about God is that he loves us.' Discuss this with a partner and compare your ideas.

**Hint** Remember to consider the other things that people believe about God as well.

# 3.4 What do people believe about life after death?

## Your lesson objectives

**In this lesson you will:**

- explore what we know about life after death

- investigate Christian beliefs about life after death

- understand the link between actions and beliefs for Christians.

## Your key words

**atonement**
Jesus' death and resurrection removed the sins of humanity and mended the relationship between people and God

**Hell**
eternal life without God

**Purgatory**
a place of purification

## What do we know about life after death?

People have always asked questions about what, if anything, happens after a person dies. There have been reports of people experiencing things such as ghosts, out-of-body experiences and being in a tunnel with a light at the end when they are near death, but the truth is that we just do not know.

This famous painting by Michelangelo in the Sistine Chapel, Vatican City is called *The Last Judgement*. What do you think it is intended to remind believers about?

## What do Christians believe?

The Old Testament teaches that being in the world is more important than looking forward to what happens after death. In the same way, in the New Testament Jesus shows through his life, teaching, healings, death and resurrection that life is to be lived fully using him as an example.

> Jesus said to her, 'I am the resurrection and the life. He who believes in me will live, even though he dies; and whoever lives and believes in me will never die.'
> (John 11:25–6)

Christians believe that death is not the end, but that after the body dies and is buried or cremated the unique soul in every human lives on. They accept that when people die they will be judged by God and treated according to how they have lived. Christians believe that judgement and fairness are important and that God will not let evil go unpunished.
They believe that God sends people to Heaven or **Hell**. Some Christians also believe in **Purgatory**.

## What do Christians believe Heaven, Hell and Purgatory are like?

### Heaven

Heaven is mentioned in the Bible but rarely described, so Christians have developed their own ideas about it. Some believe Heaven is a physical place, while others accept that it is where souls live on in a state of union with God. It is generally accepted to be a paradise where the good are rewarded.

### Hell

The Bible is even less specific about Hell. Some believe it is a place of suffering and separation from God, others accept that it is the spiritual state of being separated from God for eternity. It is traditionally associated with pain and torture.

### Purgatory

Purgatory is mostly a Roman Catholic idea. It is thought to be a place of purification for those who have died and are waiting to go to Heaven. They believe the soul needs to be cleansed from sin before it can go to Heaven.

## Why are actions important for Christians?

Christians believe that there is a strong relationship between their actions and judgement after death. Many believe that their actions in life are what God will look at to determine if they deserve to be rewarded in Heaven or punished in Hell. Christians will be aware of this in their daily lives and try to please God by living as he intended. However, they also believe in **atonement** for their sins, as they believe that God is merciful and forgiving towards those who are sorry. This is shown in the Parable of the Sheep and the Goats (Matthew 25).

### Your discussion

'We shouldn't worry about the afterlife as we don't even know if there is anything to worry about.' Do you agree with this statement?

## Learning about religion

1  Summarise what Christians believe about the afterlife.

2  Create a drawing showing Christian ideas about the afterlife.

3  Write a paragraph explaining the relationship between beliefs, actions and the afterlife according to Christianity.

# 3.4 What do people believe about life after death?

### Bahá'í
Bahá'ís believe that the soul does not die but lives for ever. When the human body dies, the soul is freed and begins its progress through the spiritual world.

### Buddhism
Buddhism teaches that death is not the end. The aim of every Buddhist is to achieve *nibbana/nirvana* – this is not seen as a place but a happy and contented state of mind.

### Hinduism
Hindus believe that the real self (*atman*) is eternal. It existed before this temporary life and survives death. The soul reincarnates through many species of life until it finds ultimate liberation.

### Humanism
Humanists do not believe there is any evidence for life after death. They believe that death is the end but that people live on in the memories of family and friends.

### Islam
Muslims believe that there will be a Day of Judgement and resurrection. Paradise and Hell are places in the afterlife where they will be rewarded or punished for what they have done in their life.

### Jainism
Jains believe every living being has an individual soul called a *jiva* that is trapped in *samsara* (the continuous cycle of rebirth). Jains believe they must aim to achieve liberation (*moksha*) – when the soul is released from *samsara* and is no longer trapped in the world.

### Judaism
Judaism teaches that at the end of time G-d will send the Messiah, a chosen spiritual leader, to save his people. Some believe that when this happens good people will be brought back to life to enjoy G-d's world and everyone will obey his rules so there will be peace.

### Sikhism
Sikhs believe in reincarnation. Each person has an eternal soul and when a person dies this provides the opportunity for reincarnation. Sikhs believe the soul experiences many lifetimes as it tries to achieve *mukti* (freedom from the cycle of reincarnation).

### Zoroastrianism
Zoroastrianism teaches that humans have a soul (*urvan*) as well as a body. On death, the human soul leaves the body and people are judged to see whether they have lived a good life and should go to Heaven or Hell.

# Drawing it all together

## Learning about religion

1 Look at two or more of the religions you have studied. Explain the differences between beliefs in reincarnation and other ideas about life after death.

2 Write a definition of these words:

afterlife

judgement.

## Learning from religion

1 Discuss with a partner what you believe about life after death. Make a list of what you agree and disagree about.

**Hint** Try to use the information you have learnt to show where your beliefs are the same or different from those of the religions you have studied.

2 Using one of the religions which believes in Heaven or Paradise, draw a picture or write a description to show what you think it would be like.

**Hint** Think carefully about this rather than just saying it would be lovely or peaceful.

3 How do you think belief in reincarnation might affect the way people behave in this life? Discuss this with a partner and compare your ideas.

**Hint** Think about how this belief might affect aspects of day-to-day living.

# 3.5 Why is belief in life after death important?

## Why is a belief in the afterlife important?

Belief in life after death helps Christians make sense of the world. A connection between the way they should live their lives and possible reward or punishment after death can give life value, meaning and purpose. Life becomes like a test, where actions have results.

It also helps some people make sense of the world in terms of good and bad experiences. At times, life can seem unfair when someone is having a hard time or suffering and it may mean that humans can understand that there is purpose to this suffering, even if they do not fully understand what the purpose is.

Belief in life after death provides support, comfort and hope that death is not the end. When a loved one has died, although it is painful, the belief that death is not the end is a help.

*The Crucifixion* by Ambrogio Borgognone, in the monastery of Certosa di Pavia Gra-Car, Lombardy, Italy.

## Your lesson objectives

**In this lesson you will:**

- investigate why belief in the afterlife is important

- explore why Christian belief in the afterlife is important

- reflect on what the resurrection of Jesus tells Christians.

## Your key words

**crucified**
fastened to a cross and left to die – a form of execution used by the Romans

**resurrected**
raised from the dead

## Christian belief in the afterlife

Christians believe that Jesus was **crucified** then **resurrected** on the third day. This means that he was raised from the dead and brought back to life by God. Resurrection is a central belief in Christianity. Christians believe that because Jesus rose from the dead they too can have a new life. Death is not seen as the end but as the beginning of a new life. Some people believe that Jesus' resurrection is also symbolic of change. It shows that anyone can start a new life if they are willing to change their ways. Life after death is a mystery and can be interpreted in many different ways.

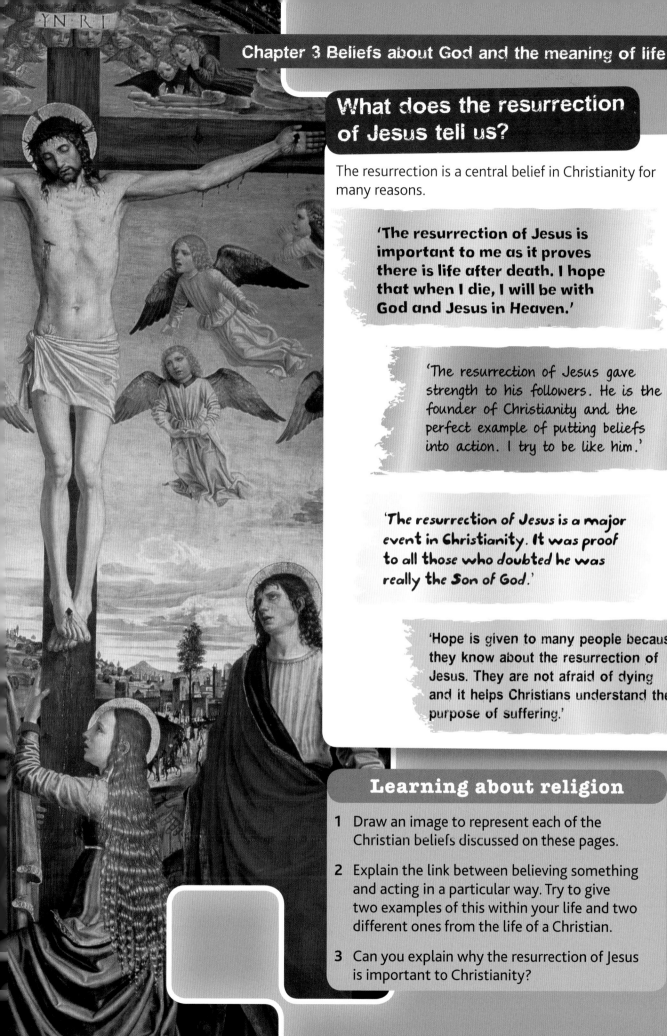

## What does the resurrection of Jesus tell us?

The resurrection is a central belief in Christianity for many reasons.

'The resurrection of Jesus is important to me as it proves there is life after death. I hope that when I die, I will be with God and Jesus in Heaven.'

'The resurrection of Jesus gave strength to his followers. He is the founder of Christianity and the perfect example of putting beliefs into action. I try to be like him.'

'The resurrection of Jesus is a major event in Christianity. It was proof to all those who doubted he was really the Son of God.'

'Hope is given to many people because they know about the resurrection of Jesus. They are not afraid of dying and it helps Christians understand the purpose of suffering.'

### Learning about religion

1 Draw an image to represent each of the Christian beliefs discussed on these pages.

2 Explain the link between believing something and acting in a particular way. Try to give two examples of this within your life and two different ones from the life of a Christian.

3 Can you explain why the resurrection of Jesus is important to Christianity?

# 3.5 Why is belief in life after death important?

## Bahá'í
In the Bahá'í Faith entry into the next life has the chance of bringing great joy. Bahá'u'lláh said that death and entry to the next life was very similar to being born.

## Buddhism
Buddhists see death as leading to rebirth unless the person has achieved *nibbana/nirvana*. Buddhists place a great deal of importance on a person being in the right frame of mind when they die since this will affect where they are reborn.

## Hinduism
Most Hindus believe in life after death and that the main purpose of human life is to achieve liberation through *yoga* (union with God).

## Humanism
Humanists do not believe in life after death. They believe that it is this life which is important.

## Islam
*Akhirah* (belief in life after death) is one of the most important beliefs in Islam. This is because Muslims believe that after death is when judgement and justice takes place and Allah rewards and punishes people for their actions in life.

## Jainism
Life after death is central to the Jain belief of a soul that is permanent. Jainism believes in reincarnation but teaches that the main purpose in life is to free the soul from the cycle of rebirth (*samsara*) and achieve liberation.

## Judaism
Jews believe that serving G-d through their actions will result in them being rewarded. They do not question what this reward will be like, they simply put their faith and trust in G-d, that he has a plan for them.

## Sikhism
Belief in life after death gives Sikhs hope that they can achieve their aim of becoming God-centred. It also reassures them that death is not the end. Belief in an afterlife gives hope and also purpose and meaning to life.

## Zoroastrianism
Zoroastrianism teaches that when a person dies their soul (*urvan*) leaves the body behind and is taken to a place of judgement called the Chinvat Bridge. Whenever a Zoroastrian makes choices, they must decide the best thing to do to ensure that their soul will be judged to be a 'good soul'.

# Drawing it all together

## Learning about religion

1 Explain why beliefs about life after death are such an important part of some of the religions you have studied.

2 Write a paragraph using the following terms and show that you understand them:

   **hope**

   **punishment**

   **reward.**

## Learning from religion

1 Imagine you are a member of one of the religions you have studied. Write a letter to a friend explaining how your beliefs about life after death affect your daily life.

**Hint** Remember you are explaining how beliefs affect your life not just saying what you believe.

2 Create a presentation which, from the viewpoint of two or more religions, tries to explain the purpose of life.

**Hint** In your presentation you will need to explain beliefs about life after death.

3 'The most important part of a religion is that it teaches that death is only a part of life.' Discuss this with a partner and compare your ideas.

**Hint** Remember to consider different religious views.

# 3.6 What makes humans different?

## Your key words

**conscience**

a knowledge of right and wrong which helps people make decisions

**DNA**

(deoxyribonucleic acid) the material in cells that contains all the 'instructions' for their development

**revelation**

something revealed that was previously hidden

**stewardship**

looking after something for someone else

## What is a human made of?

This is a challenging question and there are a number of answers depending on how the question is interpreted. A biological interpretation may say that the body is made up of organs, bones, muscles, tissue and blood. A chemical interpretation may argue that the body is made up of chemicals such as magnesium, potassium and water. The bigger question, perhaps, is what are certain parts of a human being such as the personality of a person – their thoughts, emotions, beliefs and ideas – made up of and where are they found in the human body?

## Are humans unique?

Many people, including religious believers, claim that the human body is unique. It is special and something that should be respected. However, humans are not unique in terms of their **DNA**. Scientists often point out that humans and chimpanzees share 99 per cent of their DNA. Some chimpanzees are able to communicate and perform tasks in the same way as humans. So does that mean that humans are not unique and that all animals are the same?

Many people argue that humans are not the same as animals. Humans have the ability to reason and think ideas through carefully, whereas many animals are seen to act on instinct. It is human nature to be inquisitive and ask questions in the attempt to understand. Also, humans have personalities, a knowledge of right and wrong (**conscience**) and intelligence, which some people claim animals do not have.

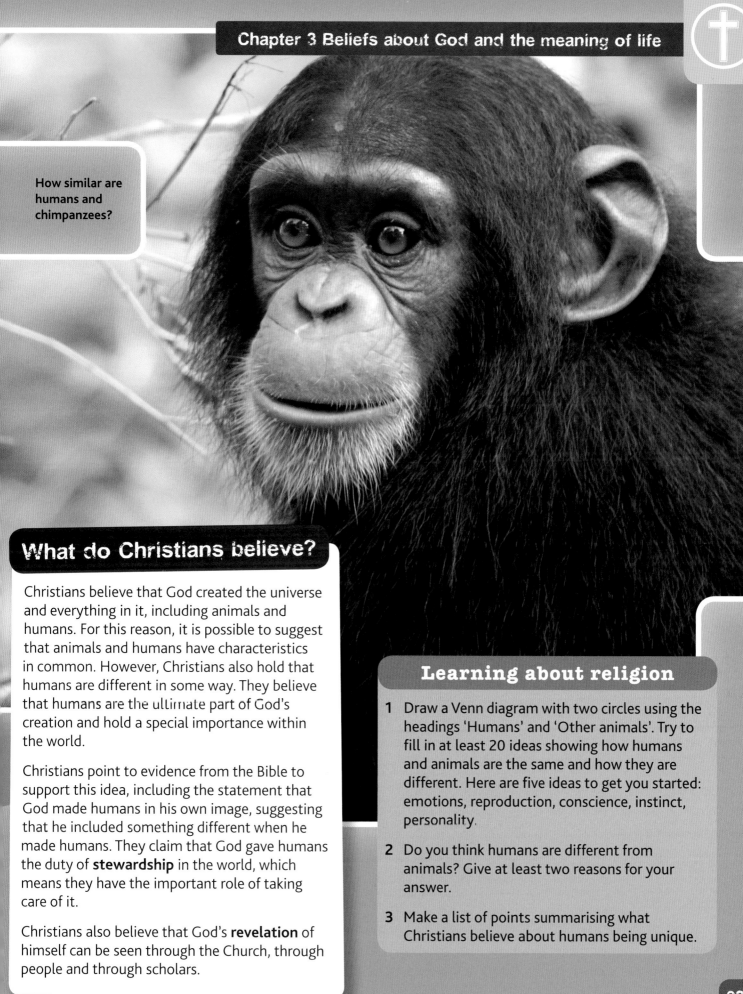

How similar are humans and chimpanzees?

## What do Christians believe?

Christians believe that God created the universe and everything in it, including animals and humans. For this reason, it is possible to suggest that animals and humans have characteristics in common. However, Christians also hold that humans are different in some way. They believe that humans are the ultimate part of God's creation and hold a special importance within the world.

Christians point to evidence from the Bible to support this idea, including the statement that God made humans in his own image, suggesting that he included something different when he made humans. They claim that God gave humans the duty of **stewardship** in the world, which means they have the important role of taking care of it.

Christians also believe that God's **revelation** of himself can be seen through the Church, through people and through scholars.

## Learning about religion

1 Draw a Venn diagram with two circles using the headings 'Humans' and 'Other animals'. Try to fill in at least 20 ideas showing how humans and animals are the same and how they are different. Here are five ideas to get you started: emotions, reproduction, conscience, instinct, personality.

2 Do you think humans are different from animals? Give at least two reasons for your answer.

3 Make a list of points summarising what Christians believe about humans being unique.

93

# 3.6 What makes humans different?

### Bahá'í
Bahá'í teachings are that the unique purpose of humans is to learn to know and love God through such methods as prayer and reflection.

### Buddhism
For Buddhists, humans have the same importance as every other living thing in the universe. However, humans are different because it is only in human form that enlightenment can be achieved.

### Hinduism
Hinduism teaches that the presence of consciousness in every living creature indicates the existence of the individual self. However, only human beings are able to exercise moral choice. This means that they are responsible for their actions and can achieve liberation from the cycle of birth and death

### Humanism
Humanists believe that there are certain characteristics which distinguish humans from other animals. These include conscience, creativity, falling In love, intelligence to know the results of their actions and right from wrong, and a sense of fairness. Other animals may have these characteristics to some extent but not as much a humans do.

### Islam
Muslims accept that humans are a special act of Allah's creation. Islam teaches that humans are a unique form of life. Muslims accept that the gifts given to humans from Allah include a soul, a conscience, knowledge and free will.

### Jainism
All life is considered sacred by Jains and they believe that all living things have a soul. Human life is considered to be the highest form of life and should be seen as special as it is only in human form that enlightenment can be achieved.

### Judaism
Jews believe that G-d created everything including humans. Humans are viewed to be the highest point of G-d's creation as Jews believe G-d made them in his image. This means that everyone can be G-d-like in their actions.

### Sikhism
Sikhs believe that God is within every soul. Humans have been given characteristics such as knowledge, understanding, morals and the ability to help others.

### Zoroastrianism
Unlike many religions which see humans as being like God's children or his servants, Zoroastrianism teaches that humans are God's helpers. Humans have a role in preventing chaos and disorder in the world.

# Drawing it all together

## Learning about religion

1 For two or more of the religions which you have studied, write down what they believe makes humans different from other animals.

2 Write a definition of these words:

   **emotional**

   **unique.**

## Learning from religion

1 Discuss with a partner what you think makes humans different from other animals. Make two lists, showing what you agree and disagree about.

**Hint** Use the information you have learnt to show where your beliefs are the same or different from those of the religions you have studied.

2 Make a list of the rights which you think all humans should have. Now go through the list and see which of these rights should apply to animals.

**Hint** Remember that some of the rights which humans have may not be suitable for animals.

3 'Humans are animals too and we should treat animals in the same way as we treat other humans.' Discuss this with a partner and compare your ideas with others in your class.

**Hint** Think about human and animal similarities and differences first and then how these will affect the way people behave towards animals.

# 3.7 What is 'the soul'?

## Your lesson objectives

**In this lesson you will:**

- understand what is meant by 'the soul'

- explore Christian beliefs about the soul.

## What is 'the soul'?

Scientists can prove that the human body is made up of bones, muscles and organs. Many claim that the body is purely a physical thing. However, many people, both religious and non-religious, would argue that there is something 'more' to every human being. They may describe it in different ways, but in the end they are suggesting that there is a non-physical element to humans. The words 'soul', 'spirit', 'mind' or 'self' may be used to describe this, but they all refer to the same thing – the part of a human that appears to be spiritual. This is the part that many people believe makes humans unique. The idea of 'spirit' is found in Genesis when God breathes life into Adam.

Rays of light are often used to represent the soul, which has no physical form that can be shown in an image.

## What do Christians believe about the soul?

Many Christians believe that humans are not just physical beings, but also have a spiritual element that makes them different from other creatures. Christians believe that the spiritual part of the body is separate from the physical part. They refer to this spiritual part as 'the soul'. Christians accept that the Bible teaches them that they were made in the image of God and that the soul is the part of a person that reflects what God is like.

Christians believe that the soul is what allows humans to communicate with God through prayer and worship. It is also the part that they believe lives on after death. Many believe that there will be a Day of Judgement when the bodies of the dead will rise and be made 'perfect' again.

## What does the Bible say about the soul?

The Bible does not say clearly what or where the soul is. There are, however, references that Christians point to when explaining their belief in the soul, for example:

> And the Lord God formed the man from the dust of the ground and breathed into his nostrils the breath of life, and the man became a living being.
>
> (Genesis 2:7)

### Your discussion

'I do not accept that humans have a soul as I cannot see it.' What arguments may be used to agree and disagree with this statement?

### Learning about religion

1 Define the word 'soul' in your own words. Use the ideas on this page to help you.

2 Summarise what Christians believe about the soul.

3 How might a Christian's belief in the existence of a soul affect the way they behave towards others?

# 3.7 What is 'the soul'?

## Bahá'í

According to Bahá'í teachings, although human beings exist on earth physically, the important part of each person is their everlasting soul. It is the soul which marks the difference between humans and other animals and grows through a person's relationship with God.

## Hinduism

Hindus believe that consciousness indicates the presence of the *atman* or real self. The *atman* is understood as eternal and unchanging. It existed before the physical body and will continue to exist afterwards. It gives life and consciousness to the body.

## Jainism

Jainism teaches that every living being from a plant to a human has an individual soul. This soul exists separately from the physical body and moves from body to body in the cycle of birth and rebirth.

## Sikhism

Sikhism accepts the idea of reincarnation where a soul (*atman*) is reborn into another body after death. The soul will go through many reincarnations in the search for *mukti* or spiritual liberation from the cycle of reincarnation.

## Buddhism

Buddhists do not accept that people have an unchanging soul. Instead, they believe in *anatta/anatman* or soul-lessness, which can be understood as a person having a spirit which changes with each rebirth.

## Humanism

Humanists do not believe that people have souls.

## Islam

Islam teaches that the soul knows everything which Allah wants it to know. The soul is the real human being and the physical body is useless without it.

## Judaism

According to Judaism, a person receives their soul when they take their first breath. The soul is believed to return to G-d after death.

## Zoroastrianism

Zoroastrianism teaches that humans were created to fight the evil spirit, Angra Mainyu. The *urvan* or soul is the part of a person that is judged for their actions and suffers reward or punishment in the afterlife.

# Drawing it all together

## Learning about religion

1 For two or more of the religions you have studied explain what they mean by 'the soul'.

2 Write a paragraph using the following terms and show that you understand them:

**mind**

**self.**

## Learning from religion

1 Choose one of the religions you have studied and compare its beliefs about the soul with a non-religious view.

**Hint** Remember to include ideas about the soul in this life and the afterlife.

2 Explain how believing they have a soul might influence a person's religious beliefs.

**Hint** Try to include a comparison with non-religious views in your answer.

3 'You have to believe in God in order to believe in a soul.' Discuss this with a partner and compare your ideas with other members of your class.

**Hint** Think about different religious views on these two beliefs.

# 3.8 The meaning of creation stories

## What do the Christian creation stories say?

The Christian stories of creation are found in Genesis, the first book of the Bible. The first one tells how God made the universe, completing his creation in six days and resting on the seventh.

- Day 1 – God separated light from darkness to make day and night.
- Day 2 – God created sea and sky.
- Day 3 – God created land, plants and trees.
- Day 4 – God created sun, moon and stars.
- Day 5 – God created fish and birds.
- Day 6 – God created humans and other animals.
- Day 7 – God rested.

Many people look at the world, see its amazing design, and believe that it must have been made by God. They believe that the complicated way in which the world works is evidence that God created and designed it. There have been many disagreements between science and religion, which are sometimes seen to be in conflict over their explanations of how the world was created. However, even some scientists believe that there is more to the creation of the world than science can explain:

> This most beautiful system [the universe] could only proceed from the dominion [lordship] of an intelligent and powerful Being.
>
> (Sir Isaac Newton 1642–1727)

## How are these stories interpreted?

Some Christians believe the creation stories are accurate accounts of what happened, while others think that they are mythical and do not believe every detail. Interpreting the creation stories does not make them any less important or true; it simply offers different understandings of their meaning.

### Your lesson objectives

**In this lesson you will:**

- understand how Christians believe the world was made
- explore how the Christian creation stories are interpreted and understood
- reflect on the importance of humanity.

① ② ⑦ ③ ④

**The Sabbath**

The days of creation according to Christianity.

## Learning about religion

1 Create a poster showing the seven days of creation. Use images to show what was created on each day.

2 According to some Christians, what is the real meaning of the creation stories?

3 Make a list of the ways in which humans are shown to be special in the creation stories.

## What is the meaning of the stories?

Many Christians believe that the true purpose of the creation stories is not to explain how the world was made, but to explain why humans exist. They believe that they contain hidden meanings about human relationships with God and their purpose on earth. Each of the following quotations tells Christians something important.

| | |
|---|---|
| You are free to eat from any tree in the garden. (Genesis 2:16b) | God cares for his creation and has provided the earth for humans. |
| Let us make man in our image, in our likeness, and let them rule over the fish of the sea and the birds of the air, over the livestock, over all the earth. (Genesis 1:26a) | God made humans with his characteristics in mind – qualities and gifts that humans should make the most of. He also gave them the earth to look after and care for. |
| Be fruitful and increase in number. (Genesis 1:28) | God wanted humans to reproduce and fill the earth with other humans. |
| God saw all that he had made, and it was very good. (Genesis 1:31a) | God was pleased with his creation and everything was just as he intended. |

# 3.8 The meaning of creation stories

### Bahá'í
The Bahá'í Faith does not have a creation story.

### Hinduism
There are many different accounts of creation in Hinduism. God is creator, supporter and destroyer. Hindus believe that time moves in a circle, with creation and destruction going on endlessly.

### Islam
The Islamic creation story is found in the Qur'an. Muslims believe that Allah created the universe in six periods of time and gave humans the responsibility to look after the world.

### Judaism
The Torah teaches that G-d is the creator of the universe and everything that exists comes from G-d. The creation stories are contained in Genesis and tell Jews that G-d created the world in six days and rested on the seventh.

### Buddhism
Buddhism is not particularly interested in questions about the creation of the universe. The teachings focus instead on life now and how to escape the cycle of rebirth.

### Humanism
Humanists do not have creation stories and accept scientific accounts of how life came to be.

### Jainism
According to Jainism, the universe was never created and will never cease to exist. It is seen as *shaswat*, which means infinite. It has no beginning or end.

### Sikhism
Sikhism is based on the idea of the unique relationship between the creator and creation. It teaches that the universe was made by Waheguru (God) speaking a single word.

### Zoroastrianism
Zoroastrians believe that the world was created by Ahura Mazda. Zoroastrianism teaches that Ahura Mazda brought the world into being in two stages. The scriptures say that he did this using his 'light' and so creation is often associated with fire in Zoroastrianism. The first stage was to create a spiritual world. In the second stage the material world was created.

# Drawing it all together

## Learning about religion

1 Looking at two of the religions you have studied, explain why creation stories are important for belief.

2 Write a definition of these words:

design

purpose.

## Learning from religion

1 Discuss with a partner whether you think there is any value in creation stories now that science has produced theories about the origins of the world.

**Hint** Think about the reasons for and purpose of creation stories.

2 Looking at the creation stories which you have studied, what common points can you find in them?

**Hint** In your answer you should also say what is different in the stories.

3 Write a passage explaining what creation stories teach about the relationship between God and humans.

**Hint** Remember to consider different religious views.

# 3.9 What are human rights?

## Your lesson objectives

**In this lesson you will:**

- learn what human rights are
- reflect on the importance of human rights
- evaluate whether everyone should have human rights.

## What are human rights?

All people agree that everyone is entitled to certain things in life. These include basic necessities which people cannot live without, such as water, food or the **right** to be cared for. This was considered to be such an important issue that, on 10 December 1948, 51 countries around the world signed a document known as the Universal Declaration of Human Rights. This document lists the rights that all humans should have and share with others, regardless of where they live, the colour of their skin or their age.

## Why was the Universal Declaration of Human Rights created?

The document was created in response to the feeling that rights need to be protected. Many people were horrified by the terrible events that took place under the Nazi administration in Germany during the Second World War, when over six million Jews were killed. It shocked people into realising that they must never let a tragedy like this happen again.

Some of the rights included in the Universal Declaration of Human Rights.

## Your key words

**injustice**
unfairness, when people are not treated correctly

**priest**
a person with the authority to perform religious ceremonies

**right**
the moral or legal claim to have or do something

## Why are human rights important?

Human rights are important to ensure that everyone receives fair treatment. Fairness and justice are two very important ideas in society. There have been many examples where the rights of people have been ignored, and this has led to suffering and even death for some people.

However, there is the question of whether everyone is entitled to the same rights. For example, should a murderer be entitled to be treated in the same way as other human beings? Whatever your answer, most people agree that it is important that humans are treated fairly.

1. All humans are born free and equal.

2. Everyone has the right to put forward their opinions.

3. Everyone has the right to freedom of thought.

4. Everyone has the right to a good education.

5. Everyone has the right to a good standard of health.

6. No one should be a slave.

7. Everyone has the right not to be tortured.

8. Everyone has the right to necessities such as food, shelter and medical care.

9. Everyone has the right to be cared for if they are sick, unemployed, old or disabled.

## What does Christianity say about rights?

Christianity teaches that every person was created equal by God and should be treated equally. Justice and fairness are at the heart of the religion and most Christians believe they should try to put principles such as 'Love your neighbour as yourself' and the Golden Rule of 'Treat others as you want to be treated' into practice. The issue of human rights is tied up with these ideas. It is about making sure that everyone is treated fairly and with respect.

Many Christians have stood up for human rights. Martin Luther King Jr is one. He was a black American who, in the 1960s, fought for equality between black people and white people. Óscar Romero is a second example; he was a **priest** who stood up against **injustice** and poor treatment of people in El Salvador, South America. Both of these men died as part of their fight for human rights.

## Learning about religion

1 Define the phrase 'human rights'.

2 Why are human rights important?

3 If you were the leader of a newly created country and had to make ten new rules for your people, what would they be and why? Share your ideas with a partner to see if they came up with similar ideas.

4 Look at the nine examples of human rights from the Universal Declaration of Human Rights. Rank them in order of importance.

# 3.9 What are human rights?

### Bahá'í
The Baha'i Faith teaches that there is only one human family and that all people share the same universal human rights. This teaching is based on the belief that all people should have dignity as part of God's creation.

### Hinduism
For Hindus, the ideal way to treat all other living beings is to identify with their feelings and have compassion. Since all beings are part of the Supreme (Brahman), their welfare should be considered in the same way as that of humans. The eternal self (soul) reincarnates until it learns this important lesson.

### Islam
Islam teaches that all humans were created equal by Allah. Muhammad ﷺ said that all people were equal like the teeth of a comb. Equality is important in Islam and Muslims believe there are basic rights shared by all humans.

### Judaism
Jews believe that, when G-d created the world, he made humans in his own image. They believe that this shows G-d made humans to be special and the most important part of his creation. As a result of this belief, Jews claim that human life is sacred and special and human rights are important for Jews.

### Buddhism
Buddhism views humans as equal, as they are all subject to the same laws of nature such as birth and death.

### Humanism
Humanists believe that they should show respect for all humans as worthy of equal consideration and support their rights for freedom of belief and expression.

### Jainism
Jains believe they should not cause harm to any living thing. They believe that every human is entitled to basic human rights. Harming anyone in any way goes against a person's human rights.

### Sikhism
Sikhism believes human life is special. The Guru Granth Sahib Ji refers to it as precious and rare. Sikhs accept that every human being, regardless of their religion, is equal and should be treated the same and fairly.

### Zoroastrianism
Zoroastrians believe that Ahura Mazda treats all persons equally and that all humans, whatever race, colour, gender, age or sex should be treated equally. Zoroastrians are taught to try to understand and accept the differences between people.

# Drawing it all together

## Learning about religion

1 Write a statement about human rights which all the religions you have studied would agree with.

2 Write a paragraph using the following terms and show that you understand them:

**equality**

**Universal Declaration of Human Rights.**

## Learning from religion

1 Working with a partner, make a list of what you think are essential human rights. You need to explain why you have chosen each one.

> **Hint** Before making your list look carefully at what the religions you have studied believe about human rights.

2 Watch some news bulletins. Make a note of each item which you think shows basic human rights being denied to someone. Now write a paragraph explaining what you think should be done about this.

> **Hint** Try to find both religious and non-religious news items.

3 'Some people do not deserve to be treated equally.' Discuss this with a partner and compare your ideas.

> **Hint** Remember to consider both sides of the argument in your answer.

# Your Assessment

Why do some religious people and non-believers think that humans are unique in the world?

> **Hint** Remember to look at two or more different viewpoints in your answer.

# 4 Good and bad

## The bigger picture

The world is full of suffering, either from natural disasters such as earthquakes and volcanoes, or from the results of people doing bad things such as lying, stealing and murdering. This chapter will explore these ideas and raise questions about the connection between good and evil, how forgiveness is possible after terrible tragedies, what can be done to help people overcome their suffering and whether the existence of suffering means that people should reconsider their understanding of God.

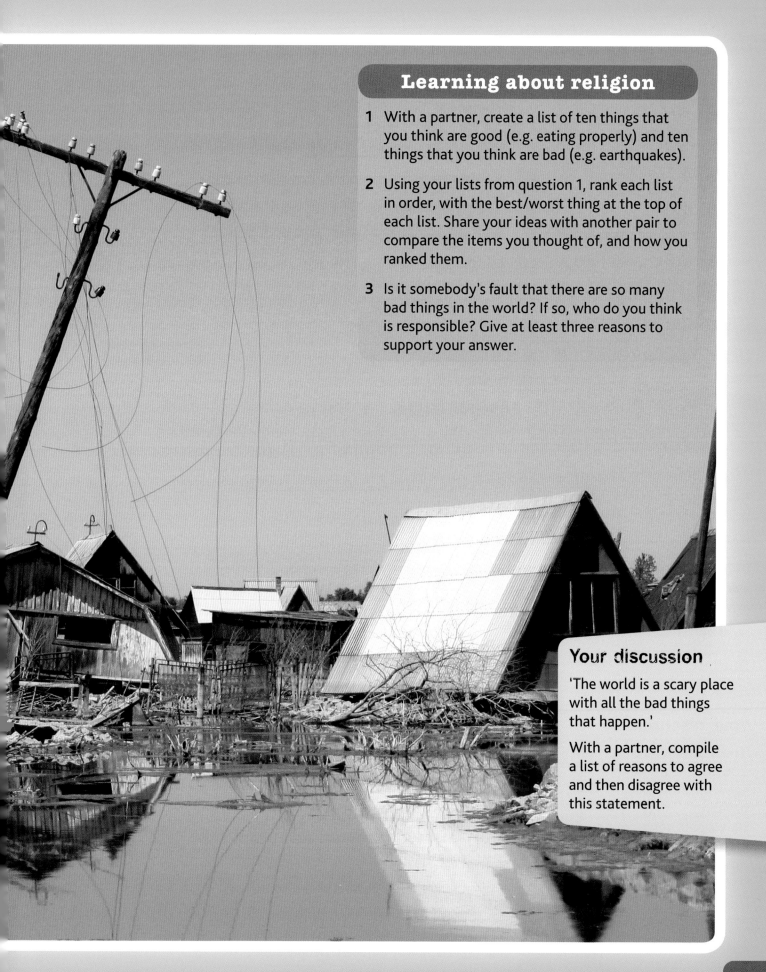

## Learning about religion

1 With a partner, create a list of ten things that you think are good (e.g. eating properly) and ten things that you think are bad (e.g. earthquakes).

2 Using your lists from question 1, rank each list in order, with the best/worst thing at the top of each list. Share your ideas with another pair to compare the items you thought of, and how you ranked them.

3 Is it somebody's fault that there are so many bad things in the world? If so, who do you think is responsible? Give at least three reasons to support your answer.

### Your discussion

'The world is a scary place with all the bad things that happen.'

With a partner, compile a list of reasons to agree and then disagree with this statement.

# 4 Introduction

# Evil and suffering

## Your lesson objectives

**In this lesson you will:**

- explore the presence of evil and suffering in today's world
- understand why the presence of evil and suffering are a problem
- begin to explore Christian beliefs about evil and suffering.

## Why are evil and suffering a problem in the world?

Evil and suffering are everywhere. You only need to turn on the television or read a newspaper to see evil acts or natural disasters and the suffering that has been caused.

### Flood destroys
Flood destroys town and then moves on

### Tragic End
Tragic end to Bonfire Night

### FAMINE KILLS
Famine claims more lives

### Jealous rage
Jealous boyfriend attacks partner

Evil is seen as deliberate actions that are intended to hurt others, and the result of evil is suffering. Evil and suffering raise many questions, both religious and non-religious.

## Your key words

**free will**
the power to act and make choices for yourself

**proof**
evidence that something is true or exists

## What questions do we have about evil and suffering?

Evil and suffering cause problems for humans because they do not understand, and may not be able to prevent, them. One question asked is why people suffer when the world is so advanced and developed. There are many other important questions concerning evil and suffering, including:

- What is the purpose of suffering?
- Does the existence of evil and suffering mean that God does not exist?
- What sort of a God would allow people to suffer?
- Are some people evil?
- Is it possible to forgive people who have done evil things?
- What can we do about evil and suffering?
- What sort of people allow others to suffer?

## Your discussion

'There cannot be a God, as if he existed he would stop evil and suffering.'
How would you respond to this statement?
How might a Christian respond? Is this the best possible world you can imagine?

These are not easy questions to answer and many people argue that there is no way to answer them. Humans struggle to understand why people suffer and especially why innocent people suffer.

Prisoners in the exercise yard at Saughton Prison, Edinburgh, Scotland. Prisoners and their families suffer as a result of their wrongdoing.

## What does Christianity say about evil and suffering?

Suffering is an important theme in Christianity. It is a challenge for many people to understand the presence of evil and suffering, especially when God is seen as being loving and powerful. Many non-religious people say that evil and suffering are **proof** that there is no God. Christians do not accept this. They believe that God gave humans **free will**. This means that they can make their own choices and decisions and can choose to do good or evil. Christians see a direct link between evil and suffering, believing that suffering is a result of human behaviour. They believe that humans need to take responsibility for their actions, as they may lead to suffering both for themselves and for others.

## Learning about religion

1 What one thing might be done in the world to help stop suffering? Discuss this with a partner.

2 Make a list of questions people have about evil and suffering. Why do you think that people cannot answer these?

# 4 Introduction
## Evil and suffering

### Bahá'í
The Bahá'í Faith teaches that evil and suffering are tests which are designed to bring people closer together through the need to help each other.

### Hinduism
Hinduism talks more about 'ignorance and wisdom' than 'evil and suffering'. It considers suffering to be an inevitable part of life in the body. It can be ended through enlightenment and liberation.

### Islam
Islam teaches that Allah is all-powerful, all-loving and all-knowing but also that Allah gave humans free will. This can explain the existence of evil in the world because it is the individual's choice to commit murder, lie or steal.

### Judaism
Judaism suggests that G-d created evil as he created everything in the world. Jews believe that G-d created evil for a purpose although people may not understand this.

### Zoroastrianism
Zoroaster taught people that they should work hard in the world to create good. By doing good things in life, people can create goodness and so fight evil and suffering. They can be good in their thoughts and words as well as their actions.

### Buddhism
Skilful and unskilful are key ideas within Buddhism. They are related to *kamma/karma*, which is the skilful or unskilful actions that a person performs in their lifetime. The Buddha identified that suffering is at the heart of the world.

### Humanism

Some Humanists choose not to use the word 'evil' because it has associations with religious beliefs and the idea of punishment for breaking rules. They believe that suffering is not a punishment for human actions but a result of human actions.

### Jainism
Jains believe that suffering occurs because of past *karma* and that doing bad deeds will bind *karma* that will cause suffering in this life or the next.

### Sikhism

Sikhs believe that although God allows evil and suffering in the world, he is not responsible for its existence. Evil and suffering do have a purpose, which is to test a Sikh's courage and faith.

# Drawing it all together

## Learning about religion

1 Looking at two of the religions you have studied, explain what they believe about suffering.

2 Write a definition of these words:

   **evil**

   **good.**

## Learning from religion

1 Discuss with a partner what you both believe about evil and suffering. Make a list of your beliefs.

**Hint** Use the information you have learnt to show how your views compare with the religious ideas you have studied.

2 Some religions believe that suffering is a test from God. Give your own opinion about whether you think God would use a test like this and why.

**Hint** In your answer you should consider different types of suffering.

3 'Suffering is not a punishment for human actions but a result of human actions.' Do you agree with this? Give examples to illustrate your answer.

**Hint** If possible, give examples from both sides of the argument.

# 4.1 What is suffering and how is it caused?

## Your lesson objectives

**In this lesson you will:**

- investigate different types of suffering
- explore what causes suffering.

## Your key words

**community**
a group of people who share something in common

## What is suffering?

Suffering can take many forms, but it is usually understood to exist when someone is in pain or distress. It can be physical, mental or emotional – these are all forms of suffering that most people experience at some point in their lives.

Distributing food to flood victims at a camp in Karachi, Pakistan, 4 October 2010. What type of suffering is shown in this photo? Do you think suffering is often seen as worse when children are involved?

## What are the different types of suffering?

Suffering can take different forms:

- suffering caused by nature, for example earthquakes, floods or other natural disasters that destroy whole **communities**, wipe out homes and kill thousands of people

- suffering where humans are responsible, such as murder and theft. This could be prevented but unfortunately often is not.

It should also be remembered that natural suffering can often be made worse by humans. For example, the effects of flooding can be made worse by people looting and taking advantage of the situation. Famine may have natural causes, but can be made worse by humans not acting to prevent it.

## Your discussion

Does suffering have some as yet unknown purpose? What do you think?

## Can we understand suffering?

Many people wonder why suffering happens. Often there seems to be no satisfactory explanation why some people suffer and others do not. Some people see a direct link between evil and suffering, with evil acts in the world causing suffering. Even if they cannot understand suffering, people can try to help themselves and others who are suffering.

## Does anyone deserve to suffer?

Do some people bring suffering on themselves? A drug addict or a criminal could be said to deserve any suffering they experience, as punishment for things they have done. However, sometimes it is not easy to break a habit, and although people may be responsible for their suffering and possibly the suffering of others whom their actions may affect, this does not really mean that they deserve to suffer.

## What do Christians say about suffering?

Christians believe that God is good and loving and cares for the universe he created. They argue that perhaps suffering has some purpose of which people are not aware. Although this might offer some explanation of suffering, it is far harder to accept that God might make people suffer, for any reason. Christians offer different explanations for suffering:

- it is a test – to see if people turn towards God in times of pain
- it is a punishment – God is punishing people for their sins
- it is part of God's plan – humans cannot fully understand God's intentions
- it is caused by humans and is the result of evil, so is not caused by God
- it is part of a world which is not perfect because humans disobeyed God (you will learn about this on page 119).

In order to try to understand suffering, Christians might also refer to particular parts of the Bible such as the Book of Job, the Suffering Servant in Isaiah and the example of Jesus.

### Learning about religion

1 Create a table with two headings – 'Natural suffering' and 'Suffering caused by humans'. Under each heading write down ten examples.

2 Why is suffering caused by humans often harder to accept?

3 Do you think there is anyone in the world who deserves to suffer? Explain your answer.

# 4.1 What is suffering and how is it caused?

## Bahá'í
The Bahá'í Faith does not say what causes suffering but teaches that all suffering has a purpose. For example, suffering can cause people to turn to God.

## Buddhism
Buddhism believes that the main causes of suffering are desire, ignorance and hatred. Buddhists recognise that humans desire pleasure and material goods they cannot have, and as these desires can never be satisfied this leads to suffering.

## Hinduism
Hindus accept that the real cause of suffering is the self's ignorance of its spiritual identity, its identification with the external mind and body, and the desire to selfishly enjoy the world through power and sensual satisfaction.

## Humanism
Humanists believe there is no god, therefore they do not think that suffering is some kind of punishment or test. They argue that, if a loving god existed, such a god could make a world without suffering.

## Islam
Islam teaches that Allah allows suffering in the world as it is a natural part of life. Muslims also believe that suffering is a test for some people to see how they react and to test their faith.

## Jainism
For Jains, suffering occurs because of past *karma*. Jainism believes that every soul is in a state of suffering. This is because each soul is part of the cycle of *samsara*, in which they are born, die and are reborn.

## Judaism
Judaism believes that we may never understand the presence of suffering in the world. Most Jews accept that it is not important to know why suffering exists, but instead to learn how best to respond to it.

## Sikhism
Sikhs accept that there is evil and suffering in the world. They believe that God did not create suffering. However, God is aware of suffering and allows it to be in the world as it tests the courage and faith of people.

## Zoroastrianism
Zoroastrians believe that evil attacks Good Creation with misery, suffering, disease and death. Before the world was created the twin spirits Ahura Mazda and Angra Mainyu had to make a choice between good and evil. Ahura Mazda chose good but Angra Mainyu did not and this brought evil into the world.

# Drawing it all together

## Learning about religion

1 Looking at two or more of the religions you have studied, explain what they believe about the cause of suffering.

2 Write a paragraph using the following terms and show that you understand them:

   natural suffering

   suffering caused by humans.

## Learning from religion

1 Draw a spider diagram. Put 'Suffering' in the middle. Add as many 'legs' with examples of suffering as you can.

**Hint** Use your own knowledge as well as religious ideas.

2 Many people have said that suffering, such as the experience of people in Africa with not enough food, is caused by the greed of others. Discuss this idea with a partner and then write a paragraph giving your opinions as well as religious views.

**Hint** You might like to focus your discussion on a particular country where people are starving.

3 'Suffering is a test.' Do you agree?

**Hint** Remember to consider religious views as well as your own.

# 4.2 Are evil and suffering connected?

## Your lesson objectives

**In this lesson you will:**

- understand the term 'evil'

- explore the story of the Fall in Genesis

- evaluate the relationship between evil and suffering.

## Your key words

**baptism**

a ceremony which cleanses a person of Original Sin and welcomes them into the Church

**Bible**

a word used for the sacred writings of the Jews (Tenakh) and Christians (Old and New Testaments)

**Original Sin**

the first sin in the world, when Adam and Eve ate from the tree that God had forbidden to them. Christians believe that all humans are born with Original Sin

**sacrament**

a religious ceremony which is the outward visible sign of an inward spiritual grace

## How are the ideas of evil and suffering connected?

Christians see a direct link between evil and suffering: suffering is the outcome of evil. When someone commits an evil act, it inevitably leads to suffering, either for the person themselves or for others. Religious leaders and the **Bible** encourage Christians to live according to Christian teachings in order to overcome evil and not cause suffering. Christians believe that God has given them the Bible to show them how to live, but that since humans have free will, they can choose whether or not to follow God's guidance. If they choose not to, they may have to accept suffering as their punishment.

*Adam and Eve in the Garden of Eden* by Wenzel Peter, Vatican Museum, Vatican City, Italy.

1 Explain your understanding of the word 'evil'.

2 Create a storyboard retelling the story of Adam and Eve and the Fall.

3 Do you think the story of Adam and Eve explains the existence of evil in the world?

4 How are the idea of evil and suffering related?

# What does Christianity say about the origin of evil in the world?

Christianity uses the story of Adam and Eve in the Book of Genesis in the Bible to explain where evil originated.

According to the Bible, God told Adam and Eve that they could eat the fruit of all the trees in the Garden of Eden, except the fruit of the tree that gives knowledge of what is good and what is evil. Life in the Garden of Eden was pleasant for Adam and Eve, and they lived happily following God's instructions.

However, one day Eve was tempted by a serpent (snake) to disobey God and eat the fruit from the tree that she knew was forbidden. She then persuaded Adam to do the same. When God realised they had disobeyed him, he punished them by throwing them out of the Garden of Eden. He told Adam that he would have to work hard to earn a living from the land, and Eve that she would suffer in childbirth, as would all women.

This story is known as the 'Fall' because it is when Adam and Eve fell from favour with God. There are different interpretations of the story. Many people associate the snake with the devil, as he tempted Eve to eat from the forbidden tree. Some Christians feel that the story is symbolic, pointing to the idea that we need to resist temptation. Others believe that the story explains the origin and meaning of the evil that is present in the world.

Many Christians believe that God created a perfect world but that the Fall brought about evil and suffering because Adam and Eve disobeyed him. Through the death and resurrection of Jesus, humanity is forgiven and brought back into a state of grace (union) with God.

Many Christians believe that because of the Fall people are born in a state of **Original Sin**, which has to be removed by **baptism**, and this is regarded as a **sacrament**.

# 4.2 Are evil and suffering connected?

### Bahá'í
The Bahá'í Faith teaches that evil and suffering are connected because when someone chooses to go against God's will they may bring suffering on themselves and others.

### Buddhism
Buddhism teaches that there is a link between unskilful actions and suffering as the unskilful actions of an individual can lead to the suffering of themselves and others.

### Hinduism
Hindus believe that evil is connected to ignorance and is related to the extent to which the soul ignores God. The soul that forgets God becomes covered in matter (according to the law of *karma*), and thus loses its natural divine qualities.

### Humanism
Humanists do not believe in a supernatural cause of evil, or that evil exists independently of people and their actions. They believe that humans are not necessarily good or evil but that they are capable of doing both.

### Islam
For Muslims, the main link between evil and suffering is humans. They believe that when Allah created humans he gave them free will. This means they can think for themselves and make their own choices, for good or bad.

### Jainism
Jains believe that bad deeds, words or thoughts bind *karma* that leads to suffering in this or the next life.

### Judaism
Judaism sees a direct link between the existence of evil and the result of suffering. Jews accept that G-d created evil but believe it was for a purpose. Although they do not understand it, they recognise that G-d would not have created evil without a reason.

### Sikhism
According to Sikhism, when humans were created God gave them free will. This was so they would be 'free' to choose to follow God rather than being forced to do so. In allowing humans to have free will, God also allowed for the presence of evil.

### Zoroastrianism
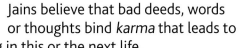
Zoroastrians believe that there are two opposing forces in the world called *asha* and *druj*. *Asha* is the law of goodness and order in the world and is the result of Ahura Mazda's creation. *Druj* is the cause of chaos and disorder and is the work of Angra Mainyu.

# Drawing it all together

## Learning about religion

1 Looking at two of the religions you have studied, explain what they believe about the connection between evil and suffering.

2 Write a definition of these words:

the Fall

temptation.

## Learning from religion

1 When people are suffering they often turn to religion for answers. Why do you think they do this?

**Hint** This question is asking for your own opinion but you should think about religious teachings and the influence they may have.

2 Write a letter to someone who is suffering because of other people's actions. Try to give them some suggestions about what might help them.

**Hint** In your letter you can use religious ideas as well as your own thoughts.

3 Most religions teach that evil and suffering are connected. Explain your own opinion about whether this is true.

**Hint** In your answer you should refer to different religious views as well as your own.

# 4.3 How do people react to evil and suffering?

## Your lesson objectives

**In this lesson you will:**

- consider how people respond to evil and suffering

- understand the ideas of forgiveness and reconciliation

- evaluate whether forgiveness is possible in all cases.

## Your key words

**faith**

belief in somebody or something especially without logical proof

**forgiveness**

no longer feeling anger or resentment towards someone who has caused you suffering

**reconciliation**

coming together again after disagreement

## How do people respond to evil and suffering?

There are many ways in which people can respond to evil and suffering. An understandable reaction is that people ask 'Why me?' and try to understand why something has happened to them. It is human nature to search for an explanation for things that people struggle to understand.

Some people may try to find someone to blame for their suffering, and religious believers may turn away from their **faith** because it cannot explain what is happening. In other cases, people may turn towards faith in times of suffering, as they receive comfort and hope from it. There is no right or wrong reaction in circumstances where someone is suffering. Christians might say that God is *in* the world but not *of* the world.

The destruction that resulted from the bomb in Enniskillen, Northern Ireland in 1987. Think about how you would feel if your home was destroyed in this way.

## Why is it so hard to understand natural suffering?

Natural suffering is due events beyond the control of humans, for example earthquakes, volcanoes or floods. The main difficulty with understanding these is that no one can be held responsible. Most Christians find it hard to believe that a good God would create natural suffering, so they cannot say whose fault it is.

## How should Christians respond to evil and suffering?

Christians believe that they should turn to their faith in times of suffering. They believe that God has given them guidance on how to prevent suffering, but many choose to ignore what the Bible says. Christians argue that the most important thing is to help those who are suffering by sharing whatever they have. Christianity also teaches about **forgiveness** and **reconciliation**.

## A brave example of forgiveness

On 8 November 1987, a bomb exploded in Enniskillen, Northern Ireland, amongst a crowd of people who were attending a Remembrance Service for people who had died in wars. Marie Wilson, a nurse who was present, was killed. Her father, Gordon Wilson, appeared on television after the bombing to talk about his reaction to the event. Instead of feeling hatred, he said:

> I have lost my daughter and we shall miss her, but I bear no ill will. I bear no grudge. ... I shall pray for those people tonight and every night.

## Learning about religion

Is natural suffering harder to explain than suffering caused by humans? Why or why not?

## Is forgiveness possible when terrible crimes have been committed?

The idea of forgiveness has gained an everyday use. People say 'sorry' when they have done something wrong and others accept their apology, forgiving them and moving on. It is harder, however, to see how forgiveness can be given in cases of human suffering where people have been killed or badly injured. Questions such as 'Is it possible to forgive?' and 'How many times?' are challenging to answer and raise questions about ourselves.

Forgiveness is an important idea in Christianity. In the Bible, Jesus spoke about the importance of forgiving others and showing mercy towards people who are sorry for what they have done. The Parable of the Lost (or Prodigal) Son (Luke 15:11–32) is an example where a father forgives his son.

### Your discussion

How easy do you think it is to forgive someone? Describe a situation where it would be easy to forgive and another where it would be difficult.

# 4.3 How do people react to evil and suffering?

### Bahá'í
Bahá'ís believe that God is all-forgiving and that they too should always be ready to forgive others

### Hinduism

In Hinduism, forgiveness is considered one of the prime qualities of a *sadhu* (holy person). God too forgives the wrongs of those who sincerely surrender to him by trying to remove or reduce the matter that has covered their souls (following the law of *karma*).

### Islam
One of the names given to Allah in the Qur'an is 'The Most Forgiving'. This shows that forgiveness is important in Islam, although it usually requires the person who has done wrong to admit their sin and be sorry for it.

### Judaism
Repentance is important in Judaism. Jews believe that repentance means that G-d will forgive them and they can move on from what happened and put it behind them.

### Sikhism
In Sikhism, forgiveness is shown to be the cure for anger. Forgiveness is also believed to be connected to compassion for the person who has done wrong.

### Buddhism
Buddhism teaches that feelings of hatred and anger towards others will leave a lasting effect on a person but forgiveness helps to overcome this. They believe that forgiving someone helps to prevent harmful thoughts and bad *kamma/karma*.

### Humanism

Humanists believe that people have the capacity for both good and evil actions and try to act in ways that show care and compassion for others. They believe it is important to forgive wrongs that have been done and try not to seek revenge.

### Jainism
Jainism stresses that forgiveness is important for the well-being of individuals and the community. However, Jains emphasise the importance of forgiveness for the person who has committed the wrong rather than the person who may have suffered. They recite a daily prayer that asks for forgiveness for harm done to any living being.

### Zoroastrianism
Zoroastrians believe that, in order to get closer to Ahura Mazda and live a good life, it is vital to perform good actions. Responding to the evil and suffering they see in the world and showing forgiveness is one way in which Zoroastrians feel they can achieve good actions. They must also expand the Good Creation by actions such as farming and having a family.

# Drawing it all together

## Learning about religion

1 Looking at two of the religions you have studied, explain what they teach about forgiveness.

2 Write a paragraph using the following terms and show that you understand them:

**blame**

**mercy.**

## Learning from religion

1 All religions teach that forgiveness is an important part of living a religious life. Why do religions see forgiveness as being so important?

**Hint** You need to think about the other beliefs that different religions hold.

2 Sometimes when someone has suffered because of someone else's actions they say that they forgive them. Explain whether you think this is the right thing to do and why.

**Hint** In your answer you need to think carefully about why someone is prepared to forgive.

3 'Suffering is good for people and makes them stronger.' Discuss this with a partner and compare your ideas.

**Hint** Remember to consider different religious views as well as your own.

# 4.4 What can be done about evil and suffering?

## Your lesson objectives

**In this lesson you will:**

- explore what can be done to limit evil and suffering

- reflect on how Christians try to reduce suffering in the world.

## Your key words

**compassion**

sympathy and care for something or someone

**injustice**

unfairness, when people are not treated correctly

**Levite**

in Judaism a person who is a member of the tribe of Levi

**priest**

a person with the authority to perform religious ceremonies

**Samaritan**

a person belonging to a religion closely associated with Judaism

## What can be done to limit the effects of evil and suffering?

Evil and suffering are significant issues in the world. Many people face a daily battle to deal with the suffering in their lives. There are things that can be done to help those who are suffering and people, both religious and non-religious, are involved in providing this help.

Many charities try to help people who are suffering as a result of natural disasters such as earthquakes or floods. Others offer support to those who are suffering due to human actions such as murder or theft.

Some people try to turn the negative aspects of their suffering into something positive. For example, in the UK a number of young people have died as a result of knife and gun crimes. Their families have tried to focus the publicity surrounding these deaths on a campaign for changes in the law and tougher penalties for those responsible.

## Why do Christians feel it is important to help those who suffer?

Christian teachings say that Christians have a responsibility to help other people. Many stories in the Bible show people such as Jesus having **compassion** for those who are suffering, and Christians believe they should try to apply the same ideas to their lives. One narrative which demonstrates this is the Parable of the Good **Samaritan** (Luke 10:30–5).

A Jew was walking along a road when he was attacked, robbed and left for dead. A **priest** and a **Levite** saw him lying there and chose to walk by without stopping. At this time, Jews and Samaritans were enemies, but when a Samaritan saw the injured man lying at the side of the road, he went to help him. The Samaritan dressed the man's injuries and put him on his own animal to take him to the nearest inn. When they arrived, the Samaritan paid the innkeeper to take care of the man. It did not matter that the Jew was his enemy, the Samaritan still showed him compassion and helped him.

## How do Christians try to help those who suffer?

Many Christian organisations try to help people who are suffering, both in the UK and all over the world. Organisations such as Catholic Agency for Overseas Development (CAFOD), Christian Aid, Tearfund, Christian Disaster Relief and World Vision are all well-known charities that provide relief such as medical care, food and water, and shelter after major natural disasters. There are many others such as Action for Children and Spurgeons. Many of them also try to educate people in developing countries so that they are more able to cope with suffering.

## How has Christian Aid helped?

Christian Aid is a Christian organisation that tries to change the world so that everyone can live free from poverty and **injustice**. It provides support and funding to many organisations in the developing world, which it calls 'partners'. Christian Aid responds in times of suffering from natural disasters, such as the floods in Pakistan in February 2010. The organisation provided funding to its partner organisations to enable them to co-ordinate food, water, shelter and medical assistance to help those who were suffering.

Christian Aid also campaigns to raise awareness of issues such as HIV and malaria and assists its partner organisations in providing medical care for sufferers. It also provides support to people in war-torn countries and speaks up for those who are not able to stand up for themselves. These are all examples of how Christian principles have been put into action to try to help those suffering in the world.

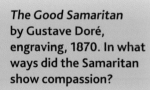

*The Good Samaritan* by Gustave Doré, engraving, 1870. In what ways did the Samaritan show compassion?

## Learning about religion

1 Write a modern-day version of the Parable of the Good Samaritan. You could make a comic strip or storyboard to illustrate your version.

2 Why do Christians feel it is important to help people who are suffering? Think of as many reasons as you can.

3 Make a list of ways in which Christian Aid has helped people overcome their suffering.

4 Research another Christian organisation that helps people who are suffering. Create a campaign poster for the organisation to get more people involved.

# 4.4 What can be done about evil and suffering?

### Bahá'í
The writings of Bahá'u'lláh stress the need to overcome suffering and predict the coming of a 'most great peace' when all people in the world will be united and live together in equality and without suffering.

### Buddhism
The Buddha taught that the way to remove desire, which is one of the causes of suffering, is to remove oneself from all worldly attachments. This belief is the third of the Four Noble Truths which contain the Buddha's teachings on suffering.

### Hinduism
Hinduism teaches that evil is overcome by transforming ourselves rather than trying to change others. By self-realisation, humans become happy, can serve others and develop all good qualities.

### Humanism
Humanists believe that human problems can only be solved by humans. They think that everyone has a responsibility to fight evil and suffering and make the world a better place to live in.

### Islam
Caring for others is seen as important to Islam – this can be seen through *zakah* (money paid annually to purify wealth) and *sawm* (fasting). All Muslims are expected to help relieve suffering by being charitable in sharing with others in their wider communities.

### Jainism
Jains believe that evil and suffering can only be overcome by achieving liberation. To do this they believe they must give up all attachments to the world. Lay Jains will give money to charity to help others, especially those who are suffering.

### Judaism
Jews believe it is important to try to fight evil, which is the cause of suffering. All humans are G-d's creation, made in his image, so Jews believe it is right to try and reduce the suffering of others.

### Sikhism
Sikhs believe that suffering is not inflicted by God but allowed by God as a test of strength and faith. They believe they should try to help others and that this will overcome suffering.

### Zoroastrianism
Zoroastrians believe that in order to get closer to Ahura Mazda and live a good life, they must perform good actions. Responding to the evil and suffering they see in the world is one way in which to do this.

# Drawing it all together

## Learning about religion

1 Looking at two or more of the religions you have studied, explain what they say about overcoming evil and suffering.

2 Write a definition of these words:

   campaign
   poverty.

## Learning from religion

1 Create a presentation showing how you think people should help those suffering in the developing world.

**Hint** Think about what the different religions teach about helping others.

2 You have been asked by a charity to produce a one-page leaflet to encourage people to give money and time to help people suffering in the UK. In the leaflet you need to give reasons why people should help.

**Hint** Include some religious and non-religious views in your writing.

3 'If everyone followed religious teachings there would be no suffering.' Discuss this with a partner and compare your ideas.

**Hint** You might like to think about how this idea could be applied on a small scale and a worldwide one.

# 4.5 Does suffering prove that there is no God?

## Your lesson objectives

**In this lesson you will:**

- identify the problems evil and suffering cause for belief in God

- evaluate religious responses to evil and suffering.

## Your key words

**atheist**

someone who believes there is no god

**belief**

accepting that something is true or real

**environment**

surroundings

**exploit**

to use another person or thing for your own advantage

**fact**

something that can be proved to be true

## What questions do people have about the existence of evil and suffering?

Many people believe religion offers answers to difficult questions such as what happens after death and how the world was made. One of the biggest unanswered questions concerns the existence of evil and suffering. People question why suffering is in our world and, more importantly, why God allows humans to suffer.

Some people take this even further by asking why good people have to suffer. It is easier to accept the idea that people who do bad things are punished, but there are many innocent people who suffer. People may also raise questions about the amount of suffering in the world as the enormous scale of what happens is hard to understand.

Is it possible still to believe in God when you see the amount of suffering in the world?

## Why is the existence of evil and suffering a problem for belief in God?

Christians believe that God is all-loving, all-powerful and all-knowing. Many **atheists** say the **fact** that there is evil and suffering in the world proves that an all-loving God does not exist. This is because it is hard to understand why a God who is all-powerful, all-loving and all-knowing seems not to do anything about the suffering of humans.

Christians believe that God loves and cares for all of his creations, including humans. They also believe God is all-powerful so could do something about the suffering in the world and all-knowing so knows how his creation is suffering. It is a challenge to try and believe in God and yet at the same time accept or try to explain why there is suffering in the world. There is a contradiction between the suffering of Jesus on the cross and an all-powerful God.

NEWS

*EARTHQUAKE DISASTER*

## Does all suffering cause problems?

For Christians, suffering caused by humans might challenge their **belief** in God. However they believe that God gave humans free will, meaning they have the freedom to choose good or evil and therefore humans are responsible for the suffering they cause, not God. Natural suffering, due to events such as hurricanes, floods, earthquakes and famine, is harder to understand as often humans do not seem to have responsibility for causing these. Questions such as why God allows these events to cause suffering are asked and there is not always a satisfactory answer offered.

## How do Christians respond to the question of whether suffering proves there is no God?

Christians do not believe that the presence of evil and suffering in the world proves that God does not exist. They have offered various explanations for why they can believe in God and accept that there is suffering in the world, such as the following.

- God may choose not to interfere in the world. He gave humans free will and so must let them use this without him interfering to change things.

- There may be a purpose to suffering, and sometimes good can be the result of suffering, for example when people work together to help others. Humans do not necessarily understand or see the full purpose.

- God knows everything about the world and knows what will happen in the future. Perhaps suffering has some long-term purpose that he is aware of but humans are not.

- Perhaps natural suffering is indirectly caused by humans. They **exploit** the earth for themselves by cutting down trees, destroying the **environment** and causing pollution. Perhaps natural suffering is partly the result of human activity and they are to blame, not God.

## Learning about religion

1 Explain why the presence of evil and suffering in the world causes a problem for belief in God.

2 Why does natural suffering cause fewer problems for some Christians than suffering caused by humans?

3 Write a conversation between an atheist and a Christian, explaining each of their views about God and the existence of evil and suffering.

4 Do you think suffering proves that there is no God? Give at least three reasons for your view.

## Your discussion

'Suffering in the world does not prove that there is no God, only that God may sometimes cause suffering for no reason and a Christian cannot believe in a God like that.'

Discuss this statement.

# 4.5 Does suffering prove that there is no God?

### Bahá'í

For Bahá'ís the existence of suffering does not affect their belief in God. They believe that God and his actions cannot be completely understood by humans but that they can understand more through prayer, meditation, fasting and charity.

### Hinduism

Hindus believe that the existence of suffering is the result of material desire and that it does not mean that God is evil or powerless. Hindus accept that the soul, a part of the Supreme, has free will. Ultimately, its own decisions and actions determine its destiny.

### Islam

Muslims believe that Allah is all-powerful and all-loving and do not question these beliefs. Muslims believe that it is free will and the ability to choose good or evil which is responsible for the suffering that can be seen in the world.

### Judaism

Jews believe that G-d has a plan for the world which humans cannot try to understand. Suffering has a purpose in the world as it can make some more faithful to their religion and is a test of their faith and belief.

### Buddhism

Buddhists do not believe in a supreme creator god. They accept that suffering comes from their own desires and ignorance and believe that people themselves have to accept responsibility for why they suffer.

### Humanism

Humanists are either atheists, who live their lives without belief in god, or agnostics, who do not believe it is possible to know whether god exists or not. They believe human beings must take responsibility for their own actions and the results.

### Jainism

Jainism does not believe that there is a creator god who made the world. Instead they believe that suffering is the result of a person's previous actions.

### Sikhism

Sikhs do not believe that God causes evil and suffering. They have no difficulty in believing in God and accepting the existence of evil and suffering.

### Zoroastrianism

For Zoroastrians, an essential part of explaining the existence of suffering is the belief in the twin spirits, Ahura Mazda and Angra Mainyu. Understanding that Ahura Mazda chose good is one of the reasons that Zoroastrians believe in him and worship him. All suffering comes from Angra Mainyu.

# Drawing it all together

## Learning about religion

1 Looking at two or more of the religions you have studied, explain what they believe about the existence of suffering.

2 Write a paragraph using the following terms and show that you understand them:

   **contradiction**

   **responsibility**.

## Learning from religion

1 Role play this with a partner. You are both religious believers. One of you has suffered badly and is questioning whether they really believe in God any more. The other is trying to help strengthen their belief.

**Hint** Make a note of your ideas before you start the role play.

2 Write a list of questions that you could ask a religious believer about how the existence of suffering affects their belief. Exchange lists with a partner and try to give full answers to the questions.

**Hint** You may want to focus your questions on the beliefs of a specific religion.

3 'If God was really all-loving he would not let people suffer.' Discuss this with a partner and compare your ideas.

**Hint** Try to refer to different religious views in your answer.

# **Your** Assessment

Summarise the ways in which religions and belief systems account for the existence of evil and suffering.

**Hint** Remember to look at two or more religions in your answer.

# 5 Rights and responsibilities

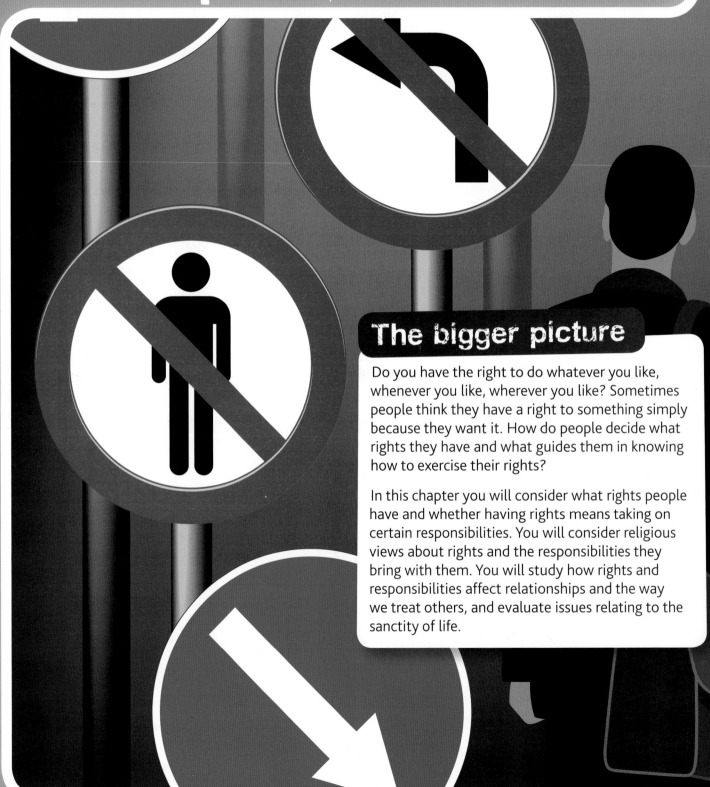

## The bigger picture

Do you have the right to do whatever you like, whenever you like, wherever you like? Sometimes people think they have a right to something simply because they want it. How do people decide what rights they have and what guides them in knowing how to exercise their rights?

In this chapter you will consider what rights people have and whether having rights means taking on certain responsibilities. You will consider religious views about rights and the responsibilities they bring with them. You will study how rights and responsibilities affect relationships and the way we treat others, and evaluate issues relating to the sanctity of life.

1 Make a list of the things you would like and the things you need. Compare and discuss your list with a partner. How many of the things on your list are things you have a right to?

2 What responsibilities do you have:

- at home
- at school
- in the community, a religious group, a youth group or a job you do?

3 How do we know:

a what is right

b what responsibilities are?

### Your discussion

Consider what might happen if everyone had the right to do exactly what they wanted.

# 5 Introduction

# What are my rights and responsibilities?

## Your lesson objectives

**In this lesson you will:**

- explore the origins and meaning of Christian teachings about free will

- consider what rights people have as human beings

- evaluate the links between rights and responsibilities.

## Your key words

**Bible**

a word used for the sacred writings of the Jews (Tenakh) and Christians (Old and New Testaments)

**conscience**

a knowledge of right and wrong which helps people make decisions

**free will**

the power to act and make choices for yourself

**opinion**

someone's personal view on a subject

**right**

the moral or legal claim to have or do something

## What do Christians believe about rights and responsibilities?

Christians believe that God created humans with **free will**, the freedom to make choices between right and wrong. The Book of Genesis in the **Bible** tells the story of how Adam and Eve used this freedom and chose to disobey God (Genesis 3:1–24). As a result, they and all their descendants were banished from the Garden of Eden and condemned to a life of hard work and suffering. However, they still had free will and the knowledge of good and evil. This story in Genesis is called the 'Fall': 'And the LORD God said "The man has become like one of us, knowing good and evil"' (Genesis 3:22a).

Most people believe that everyone has the right to life and to live in freedom and safety. Do people take their rights for granted?

# Do rights bring responsibilities?

After the Second World War (1939–45) 51 countries, including Britain, joined an organisation called the United Nations and worked together to create an agreement about the basic **rights** of every human being in the world. This is called the Universal Declaration of Human Rights. Christians were actively involved in drawing up the Declaration, which emphasises that rights bring responsibilities to ourselves and to others, and that everyone should respect others and be respected:

> All human beings are born free and equal in dignity and rights. They are endowed with reason and conscience and should act towards one another in a spirit of brotherhood. (Article 1)

> Everyone has the right to freedom of opinion and expression; this right includes freedom to hold opinions without interference and to seek, receive and impart information and ideas through any media and regardless of frontiers. (Article 19)

> Everyone is entitled to a social and international order in which the rights and freedoms set forth in this Declaration can be fully realized. (Article 28)

Children on a rubbish tip in Antananaviro, the capital of Madagascar. How would you feel if you had to work like this?

## Learning about religion

1  What do Christians mean by 'free will'?

2  Read the story of the Fall in Genesis. Why do you think it as known as the 'Fall'?

3  Look at the picture above.

   a Describe what is happening in the picture.

b What has caused this situation?

c When some people exercise what they feel are their rights, can it result in others losing theirs? Give some examples.

4  What responsibilities do you think you have towards other people?

# 5 Introduction
# What are my rights and responsibilities?

## Bahá'í
Bahá'ís believe that the world should be run as if it were one country where everyone is treated equally and fairly. All Bahá'ís have the responsibility to try to make sure that no one goes hungry and that there is lasting peace.

## Hinduism
Hindus believe that others' rights are respected when humans perform their *dharma* (duty) towards God, the great sages, elders, family members and all living creatures.

## Islam
The Qur'an teaches Muslims about the importance of respecting the rights of others and treating them justly. Muslims believe they have a responsibility to care for and protest all of Allah's creation.

## Judaism
Judaism teaches that G-d wants people to work for justice and the rights of others. Jews believe they have a responsibility to care for others and to protect G-d's creation.

## Sikhism
Sikhs believe that rights bring responsibilities. They follow a Code of Conduct which sets down their moral and spiritual responsibilities to God, themselves, others and God's creation. Those who do not follow it cannot be referred to as a 'Sikh'.

## Buddhism
Buddhists believe that all life is interconnected and all actions have results for themselves and others. They believe that they have a responsibility to put the *Dhamma/Dharma* – the Buddha's teachings – into practice.

## Humanism
Humanists believe everyone has the right to a fulfilled and happy life. They emphasise that rights bring responsibilities to themselves and to others and that everyone should respect others and be respected.

## Jainism
Jains believe strongly that all life is connected and should not be harmed and that they must defend the rights of those who cannot help themselves. Jains believe they have responsibilities towards people, animals and the environment.

## Zoroastrianism
Zoroastrians believe that humans have a responsibility to help God to keep his creation pure and free from evil. To do this they follow three commandments: to practise good thoughts, good words and good deeds.

# Drawing it all together

## Learning about religion

1 Read through the teachings of the different belief systems about rights and responsibilities. In all cases there is a belief that rights bring with them certain responsibilities. List all the responsibilities then analyse your list to identify how many are specifically religious. Do you need to be religious to be a responsible person? If not, what would make you decide?

2 Look carefully at the extracts from the Universal Declaration of Human Rights on page 137. Choose which one you think is most important and explain why.

## Learning from religion

1 What rights do you have at this point in your life? What rights will you gain as you grow older? Do you think that having rights means you have to take on responsibilities? Give your reasons.

**Hint** Start by thinking about the things you are allowed to do now and things you are not allowed to do because you are not old enough.

2 Would you describe yourself as a responsible person? Why/why not? What responsibilities do you have? Do you actually carry them out? Do you enjoy having responsibility?

**Hint** Try to be honest when you think about your answers to this question. Share your answers with a partner and see whether they agree with your view of yourself.

3 Imagine that the Bahá'í vision that the world was run as one country came true. Do you think it could ever work? What would be the advantages and disadvantages?

**Hint** Think about such things as having one world language and one world currency, a world police force and no armies.

# 5.1 What does religion teach about rich and poor?

## Your lesson objectives

**In this lesson you will:**

- consider Christian teaching about the responsible uses of money

- analyse the way Christian beliefs about money affect how Christians live their lives

- reflect on your own attitudes to poverty and wealth and the use of money.

## Your key words

**community**

a group of people who share something

**covet**

want to possess something

**eternal life**

life after death

**exploit**

to use another person or thing for your own advantage

**injustice**

unfairness, when people are not treated correctly

**stewardship**

looking after something for someone else

## What does Christianity teach about rich and poor?

Christians try to put into practice Jesus' teaching that they should love their neighbour as much as they love themselves (Mark 12:30). This means that they have a responsibility to make the world a fairer place where resources are more equally shared. Christians believe they must take positive action to fight against poverty and social **injustice** anywhere in the world, so many of them give a proportion of their income to support charities such as Christian Aid, Catholic Agency for Overseas Development (CAFOD) and Tearfund.

## What attitudes do Christians have towards money?

In their daily lives, Christians try to obey the commandment that says they should not **covet** the lifestyles and possessions of others (Exodus 20:17). The first Christian **communities** were formed in the first century CE; they lived simply and shared their possessions (Acts 2:44–5). People who live in Christian religious communities today still live in this way. St Paul wrote about the dangers of misusing money in a letter to his friend Timothy, saying, 'For the love of money is a root of all kinds of evil' (1 Timothy 6:10a). Christians believe they must earn their living honestly, in ways that do not harm or **exploit** others.

When Jesus was asked by a rich ruler what he needed to do to gain **eternal life**, Jesus told him he must sell everything and give all the money to the poor. The man went away: the one thing he felt he could not do was give up his wealth (Luke 18:18–25). Most Christians do not criticise the accumulation of wealth but the ways in which wealth is often used. The use of wealth is part of Christian **stewardship**.

The actress Lucy Liu attends a grand opening at the Swarovski Crystallized Concept Store, New York, 2009.

## Learning about religion

1 How easy is it to live without coveting what other people have? What sort of things do you covet?

2 What sort of things might St Paul have been thinking about when he wrote that loving money is the cause of evil in the world? Do you agree with him? Explain your reasons.

3 How do you think the rich ruler felt after his conversation with Jesus?

4 If you were a millionaire for a day, what would you do with your money?

A homeless person begging for money on a London street, 2009. Can we really say that money is always bad?

# 5.1 What does religion teach about rich and poor?

### Bahá'í
Bahá'ís believe they are developing their souls to be ready for the next world and so must earn and use their money in ways that are honest and helpful and do not harm or exploit others.

### Buddhism
Buddhists believe that wealth might be the result of being generous in a past life. They think money should be used to help others and reduce suffering due to discontent (*dukkha/dukha*).

### Hinduism
Hinduism teaches that there are two great evils: greed and poverty. Both drive humans to focus on money. Wealth should be used in service. Many saintly people renounce personal wealth.

### Humanism
Humanists do not think money is bad. What matters is how it is used. Humanists think that as we are all part of the same species we have a responsibility to help others.

### Islam
Muslims do not believe money is bad but that it must only be used in good ways. Lending money at interest, gambling and lotteries are not allowed.

### Jainism
Jains try to live without attachment to material wealth and possessions. They believe they should cause the least possible harm, therefore money must be earned and used in a good way.

### Judaism
Judaism teaches that all business deals must be done honestly. Jews think that one of the best ways of helping others is to lend money at no interest.

### Sikhism
Sikhs believe that money must be earned honestly and used well. They think that gambling, lending and borrowing are not good uses of money.

### Zoroastrianism
Zoroastrians believe that humans can choose to act for good in the world and to fight against evil, therefore they should choose to use money in ways which will result in good rather than harm. Charity is a major duty for Zoroastrians.

# Drawing it all together

## Learning about religion

1 Take two of the religions you have learnt about and write two sentences summarising what each one teaches about the uses of money. What are the similarities and differences between the two views?

2 Think about the teachings of the religions you have studied about the use of money. Do you think it is possible to be very rich and still be true to your religious beliefs? Explain your views.

## Learning from religion

1 Do you agree with the Humanist view that, because we are all part of the same species, living together on the same planet, everyone has a responsibility to help the poorest people? Why/why not?

**Hint** Remember that Humanists do not believe in a god or gods and make their decisions based on their understanding of what will improve the quality of life for most people.

2 How might believing that you will be reborn into another life affect the way you use your money in this life?

**Hint** In your answer you need to think about what people believe about *kamma* or *karma*.

3 Do you think that lotteries are bad uses of money? Why do you think so many religions are against this way of using money?

**Hint** Make sure you weigh up the possible benefits that could result from a lottery as well as the possible harm.

# 5.2 Should we help others?

## How many people need help?

There is a big gap between the richest and the poorest people in the world today.

According to the United Nations, about 25,000 people, many of them children, die every day from hunger, despite the fact that there is enough food in the world to feed everyone. Causes of poverty include poor harvests, war, natural disasters such as floods, and world debt. People of all religions believe they should do all they can to try to make the world a better, fairer place.

## What do Christians believe about helping others?

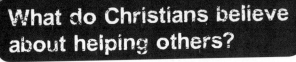

Christians believe they have a duty to help people who are in need or **oppressed**. They believe that Jesus' teaching in the Parable of the Sheep and the Goats in Matthew 25 means that people will be judged according to how well they have cared for others. Jesus taught that people should obey the commandment 'Love the Lord your God with all your heart and with all your soul and with all your mind and with all your strength' (Mark 12:30) and that this leads to the second commandment 'Love your neighbour as yourself' (Mark 12:31a).

Jesus made it clear that he had come to earth to support and bring hope to the poorest members of society:

> The spirit of the Lord is on me, because he has anointed me to preach good news to the poor. He has sent me to proclaim freedom for the prisoners and recovery of sight for the blind, to release the oppressed.
> (Luke 4:18)

Christians believe that they must follow Jesus' teaching and take positive action against poverty and unfair treatment. Many give a proportion of their income to charities such as Christian Aid or Catholic Agency for Overseas Development (CAFOD). Others give their time to help in, for example, charity shops or homeless shelters.

Homeless people in Tokyo. What kind of help are they receiving?

## Learning about religion

1 Why do Christians believe they should help others?

2 How do Christians help people in need?

3 How would you respond to someone who said, 'I don't give to charity. It's not my fault if people are poor'?

# 5.2 Should we help others?

### Bahá'í
Bahá'ís believe the soul is being developed ready for the next world and needs to gain good qualities such as care and compassion for others. Bahá'ís try to treat others with care and kindness.

### Hinduism
Hindus believe that all living beings exist to serve. Humans should give wealth to good causes and to promote enlightenment. Money should not support ignorance or other forms of harm.

### Islam
The Qur'an teaches Muslims to share their money with the poor. Muslims pay *zakah*: the duty of each person to make payment of an annual contribution which purifies their wealth and is given to those who are entitled to receive it.

### Judaism
The Torah teaches that Jews must give a portion of their income to the poor. This is called *tzedaka* which means 'righteousness'.

### Buddhism
The Buddha taught that material wealth does not bring happiness but Buddhists believe they should give to help others meet their basic needs.

### Humanism
Humanists try to live by the Golden Rule, treating others as they would like to be treated. Humanists think that the fact that we are all human beings means that we have a responsibility to help those in need.

### Jainism
Jains believe that all human beings should be compassionate and help each other, as everyone depends on each other for survival.

### Sikhism
Sikhs believe it is the responsibility of the rich to look after the poor. They give their time and talents as well as money to help others.

### Zoroastrianism
Zoroastrians believe they should live by good thoughts, good words and good deeds. They work to improve their communities and give generously to charities. They also have a duty of care for animals and the natural world.

# Drawing it all together

## Learning about religion

1 Choose two religions you have studied and write a sentence for each of them explaining why a member of that religion might give money to a charity.

2 Make a list of at least four ways someone might help people in need.

## Learning from religion

1 What differences would it make to your life if you lived by good thoughts, good words and good deeds? Do you think it is possible to live in this way? Why/why not?

**Hint** Try and separate thinking, speaking and doing to help you answer this question.

2 Do you need to be religious to care about other people? Why/why not? Make a list of things you have done to help others. Why did you do them?

**Hint** Remember to include projects you have been involved in at school, raising money for charities for example, and things you do to help out at home, even if they are things you do not really want to do.

3 Ask the people in your class or group the question 'Should we help others? Why/why not?' Note down their answers.

**Hint** Do this as a whole class activity and analyse and discuss the findings of your survey, drawing conclusions based on your research.

a What sort of reasons did people give?

b Were they selfish reasons?

c Were any of them based on religious beliefs?

# 5.3 Why are some people prejudiced?

## Your lesson objectives

**In this lesson you will:**

- consider what prejudice is and how it affects people

- explore Christian attitudes to prejudice.

## Your key words

**apartheid**
separation into different racial groups

**discrimination**
treating someone unfairly because they belong to a particular group or class

**faith**
belief in somebody or something especially without logical proof

**homophobia**
prejudice against homosexuals and/or homosexuality

**oppression**
cruel or unjust treatment

**prejudice**
an opinion formed without knowledge or reason

## What is prejudice?

To show **prejudice** is to prejudge someone or something without knowing all the necessary facts. Prejudice can lead to **discrimination** and unfair treatment. Christians believe that everyone is equal in the eyes of God. The teaching of Jesus is based on love: 'A new command I give you: Love one another. As I have loved you, so you must love one another' (John 13:34). Jesus taught that people should love other people, even their enemies.

## How do Christians challenge prejudice?

Many Christian men and women have challenged prejudice and unfairness. Desmond Tutu was the first black bishop in South Africa and was awarded the Nobel Peace Prize in 1984. He has a deeply held belief that everyone is equal and has spent his life speaking out against what he believes is unfair treatment. He fought against **apartheid** in South Africa and has campaigned against **homophobia**, the **oppression** of women, poverty and racism:

> You are either in favour of evil or you are in favour of good. You are either on the side of the oppressed or on the side of the oppressor. You can't be neutral.

(Speech to the US House Foreign Affairs Subcommittee on Africa in 1984)

Although retired, Bishop Tutu is still campaigning for justice and human rights and has great **faith** in the power of young people to change the world.

Talking to young people, Bishop Tutu has said: 'Just go on dreaming that we can have a different kind of world.'

## Learning about religion

1   Summarise Christian teaching about how people should treat each other.

2   What does Desmond Tutu mean when he says 'You can't be neutral'? Do you agree? Why/why not?

3   Can young people change the world? If so, where should they start?

149

# 5.3 Why are some people prejudiced?

### Bahá'í
Bahá'ís believe in unity. They believe all human beings should be like one family. Everyone should be treated with love and kindness and without prejudice because of their race or religion.

### Buddhism

For Buddhists discrimination of any kind is unacceptable. Buddhists believe men and women are spiritually equal. They work to promote understanding between religions.

### Hinduism
Many Hindus believe that it is wrong to discriminate against someone because of their race or gender. Hindus believe that people of different religions should respect each other.

### Humanism
Humanists believe people should be treated as individuals. They do not agree with stereotyping and discriminating against people. Humanists think the world would be a better place if everyone treated people of all kinds with respect.

### Islam
Muslims believe that Allah created all people equal. Muhammad ﷺ taught that there should be no discrimination on grounds of race or colour.

### Jainism

Jains believe people have many different viewpoints and that they should try to look at things from others' points of view, showing tolerance to different religions and ways of life.

### Judaism
Jews believe that everyone is descended from Adam and all are equal in the eyes of G-d, whatever their beliefs.

### Sikhism

Sikhs regard everyone as equal regardless of religion, race or gender. They believe everyone should be free to practise their religion.

### Zoroastrianism

Zoroastrians believe that men and women, rich and poor, young and old are all equal. The only way one person can be better than another is in terms of their righteousness.

# Drawing it all together

## Learning about religion

1 Write a paragraph using the following words to show that you understand what religious people think about these ideas:

**stereotyping**

**prejudice**

**discrimination.**

2 Make a list of as many different forms of prejudice and discrimination as you can. How do you think one of the religions you have studied should respond to these?

## Learning from religion

1 Why are people prejudiced? Are they born prejudiced or do they become prejudiced? Give reasons for your views.

**Hint** Think carefully about what prejudice means and how it might develop.

2 How would you react if you or one of your friends was bullied for racist reasons?

**Hint** It might help if you try putting yourself in the shoes of someone who has experienced bullying of this kind. What might it feel like?

3 List five things ordinary people could do to stop prejudice developing. Share your list with a partner and combine your best ideas into one list.

**Hint** Bring your ideas together and discuss them as a class to see how you might put some of them into practice in your school or community.

# 5.4 Is life sacred?

## Your lesson objectives

**In this lesson you will:**

- explore what is meant by 'sacred'

- evaluate Christian beliefs about the sanctity of life.

## Your key words

**abortion**

the deliberate ending of a pregnancy by removal and destruction of the foetus

**belief**

accepting that something is true or real

**contraception**

the deliberate use of methods to prevent pregnancy

**divine**

coming from God

**euthanasia**

literally, an 'easy' or 'gentle' death: ending a life painlessly to relieve suffering

**Heaven**

a place of paradise and reward in the presence of God

## Why do Christians believe life is sacred?

Christians believe that human life is **sacred**. This **belief** in the **sanctity of life** influences their views about issues such as **abortion**, **euthanasia** and the care of older people and people who are disabled. Christians believe that all life is a gift from God and that God created humans in his image (Genesis 1:27). This does not mean that humans actually look like God, but that they are special. The **Quaker** George Fox (1624–91) described this as a 'divine light' and taught that there is 'that of God' in everyone.

The poet William Wordsworth wrote about a newborn baby as having come from God:

Not in entire forgetfulness,
And not in utter nakedness,
But trailing clouds of glory do we come
From God, who is our home:
Heaven lies about us in our infancy!
(from 'Ode: Intimations of Immortality')

The belief that life is sacred leads many Christians to oppose anything that interferes with the natural processes of life and death, such as abortion and euthanasia. Other Christians feel that provided they are guided by the principle of 'unconditional love' then it is correct to interpret this for different situations. Some Christians feel the same way about artificial methods of **contraception**. They believe that the beginning and end of life are the responsibility of God. However, most Christians would agree with the use of other methods of family planning. Christians often quote from the book of Ecclesiastes in the Old Testament of the Bible to illustrate their belief that the pattern of life follows God's purpose:

There is a time for everything,
and a season for every activity under heaven:
a time to be born and a time to die,
a time to plant and a time to uproot.
(Ecclesiastes 3:1–2)

'Heaven lies about us in our infancy!'

## Learning about religion

1  How might their belief that life is sacred influence Christians' views about abortion and euthanasia?

2  What do you think George Fox meant when he said there is a 'divine light' in everyone?

3  Why do you think William Wordsworth described a new baby as 'trailing clouds of glory'?

### Your key words

**Quaker**
a member of the Christian denomination otherwise known as the Religious Society of Friends

**sacred**
considered to be special and holy

**sanctity of life**
the belief that life is sacred or holy

# 5.4 Is life sacred?

### Bahá'í
Bahá'ís believe that all life is sacred because everything was created by God. They believe every person has the potential to develop their soul so that it reflects the qualities of God.

### Buddhism
Buddhists believe that all life is sacred and that all forms of life are connected. Buddhists practice *ahimsa*, non-violence, and try to live in a way that does good rather than harm, showing loving kindness and compassion to humans and animals.

### Hinduism
Hindus see all life in terms of the soul or consciousness (*atman*), not the external signs such as eating, breathing and reproducing. The principle of *ahimsa*, non-violence towards all living creatures, shows that all life is considered to be sacred.

### Humanism
As Humanists do not hold religious beliefs they do not think life is sacred. They believe that all people have the right to live a happy and fulfilled life where everyone is respected and respects others.

### Islam
Muslims believe that Allah created the world and everything in it and all life belongs to Allah. All life is sacred or holy because it was created by Allah. They believe everyone has something of God in them.

### Jainism
*Ahimsa* (non-violence) is central to Jain beliefs. They believe that all life forms are sacred and have a soul. They should try to minimise harm to all living beings whether they are humans, animals, microbes or plants.

### Judaism
Judaism teaches that G-d created the world and that men and women were created in the image of G-d. Jews believe that life is a sacred gift from G-d.

### Sikhism
Sikhs believe that all life is sacred and holy because it was created by God. They believe that God is immanent, which means he is in every human being.

### Zoroastrianism
Zoroastrians believe God created both the visible and invisible worlds from his own body and his own light. They believe human beings have a spiritual as well as a physical part and share the spiritual qualities of God. All that God created is sacred: people, plants and animals.

# Drawing it all together

## Learning about religion

1 Explain what religious people mean when they say that life is 'sacred'.

2 Some religious people believe that there is something of God in all human beings. If people believe this, how might it affect the way they treat others?

## Learning from religion

1 If you believe that life is sacred are you more likely to treat others in a decent and respectful way? Why/why not?

**Hint** Remember to look at religious and non-religious views in your answer.

2 Do you think humans have a spiritual as well as a physical part?

**Hint** The word 'spiritual' often refers to the aspects of humans which relate to their feelings, beliefs and emotions.

3 Many religions believe that there is a goal or purpose to human lives. Do you agree with this? If so, what do you think that goal might be?

**Hint** It would help to write down your ideas and share them with a partner or discuss them as a class before you tackle this question.

# 5.5 What do religious people believe about relationships?

## Your lesson objectives

**In this lesson you will:**

- identify key Christian teachings about relationships

- evaluate the impact of their beliefs about relationships on the lives of Christians today.

## Your key words

**adultery**

a sexual relationship between a married person and someone to whom they are not married

**denomination**

a branch of a religion

**promiscuous**

having many casual sexual relationships

**sacrament**

a religious ceremony which is the outward visible sign of an inward spiritual grace

**virgin**

a person who has not had sex

## What do Christians believe about sexual relationships?

St Augustine taught that sex was a gift from God to be enjoyed by a man and a woman within marriage and to enable them to have children. Many Christians believe that men and women should remain **virgins** until they are married. They also believe that **adultery** is wrong because it involves breaking vows made before God and promises made to another human being. The seventh commandment states 'You shall not commit adultery' (Exodus 20:14). Adultery is a betrayal of the trust and love in a relationship. The Roman Catholic Church teaches that sex outside marriage is always 'a grave sin' (Catechism of the Catholic Church, paragraph 2390).

Many liberal Christians such as Quakers believe Jesus taught that love is what matters most and that the quality of a relationship is the most important thing. They believe that couples can choose to live together in a loving relationship without being married and also that some people may choose same-sex relationships.

Christian views about the use of contraception differ. The Roman Catholic Church forbids all methods of artificial birth control and teaches that sex should always be open to the possibility of God's gift of a baby. Most Protestant Christians accept the use of contraception in marriage, recognising that people may want to plan the timing of pregnancies to ensure that all their children are wanted children. However, some Christians are concerned that using contraception outside marriage may lead to **promiscuous** behaviour.

Most Christians believe that marriage should last for a lifetime and promise to stay together 'until death us do part'. Although no Christian **denomination** approves of divorce, most recognise that it is sometimes inevitable especially as people live longer. Divorce is allowed by Protestant and Orthodox Christians, but the Roman Catholic Church teaches that marriage is a **sacrament** that can be ended only by God.

How can schools prepare young people for the challenges of adult relationships?

## Learning about religion

1 Explain why some Christians accept contraception while others do not.

2 This extract from the first of St Paul's letters to the Corinthians is often read at Christian weddings:

Love is patient, love is kind. It does not envy, it does not boast, it is not proud. It is not rude, it is not self-seeking, it is not easily angered, it keeps no record of wrongs. Love does not delight in evil but rejoices with the truth. It always protects, always trusts, always hopes, always perseveres. Love never fails.

(1 Corinthians 13:4–8a)

a Why do you think many Christian couples choose the extract from 1 Corinthians 13 to have read at their wedding? How might it help them during their marriage?

b Write your own version of the passage from 1 Corinthians 13, beginning each line with the words 'Love is …'. Share your work and put together a class version.

# 5.5 What do religious people believe about relationships?

### Bahá'í
Bahá'ís believe that human sexuality is a gift from God and that in marriage the couple are joined in body and spirit. Divorce is disapproved of but is not banned.

### Buddhism
Buddhists believe relationships should be based on love and compassion not lust. Faithfulness is expected in marriage. Buddhists accept divorce if a marriage fails but believe the least harm possible should be caused.

### Hinduism
Hinduism discourages sex outside of marriage. In household life, men and women have different roles and duties. Many marriages are arranged by family elders. In modern times, divorce is often allowed although rarely encouraged.

### Humanism
Humanists believe all relationships should be based on mutual respect. Marriage is a serious commitment based on shared responsibility. The couple choose the words they will say and often share aspirations rather than make vows or promises.

### Islam
Muslims have strict rules about sexual relationships which must only take place within marriage. Many marriages are arranged. Divorce is allowed if a marrige breaks down but is not encouraged.

### Jainism
Jains try to achieve peace and harmony and avoid mental and physical violence in all their relationships. They believe marriage is very important and that couples should love each other selflessly. Jains do not encourage divorce.

### Judaism
Jews believe that sex should only take place in marriage. The marriage contract in which the groom promises to look after his bride is important. Jews believe marriage should be for life but divorce is allowed.

### Sikhism
Sikhs believe marriage is a sacred bond which should be for life. The Sikh wedding service emphasises the union of two souls. Divorce is permitted if a marriage fails.

### Zoroastrianism
Zoroastrians believe that marriage is the strongest link in the chain that binds human beings together. They believe that the most important relationships in life come from marriage: husband/wife, parents/children, brother/sister.

# Drawing it all together

## Learning about religion

1 Choose two religions you have studied and write a sentence to summarise each of their teachings about marriage and divorce.

2 Why do you think that religions stress the importance of marriage so much?

## Learning from religion

1 Write down the most important qualities you think are needed to make good relationships and then rank them in order of importance.

**Hint** Think carefully about your own experiences of what makes relationships work, with your friends for example.

2 What is the difference between aspirations and vows or promises? Are aspirations enough as the basis for a marriage?

**Hint** An aspiration is something someone aims or hopes for.

3 In 2008, over 120,000 couples in the UK divorced. Do you think couples should make vows to each other when they marry? Why/why not?

**Hint** Think carefully about why people might be willing to make promises that may be difficult to keep.

# 5.6 What is abortion?

## What is abortion?

Abortion is the deliberate ending of a pregnancy by removing and destroying the **foetus**. More than 200,000 women in the UK have abortions every year. Around 4000 of these are girls aged under 16, the legal age of consent for sex. In the UK, abortions are legal if the foetus is less than 24 weeks old, as long as two doctors agree to the abortion. An abortion has to be carried out before the baby could live outside the womb without medical help. Abortions over 24 weeks are only allowed in exceptional circumstances, for example if the mother's life is in danger, if there is a high risk that the baby will be born with a serious disability, or if a woman has become pregnant as the result of **rape**.

Anti-Abortion and Pro-Life law demonstration, Georgia State Capitol building, Atlanta, USA. Many people have strong views about abortion because of their religious beliefs.

## What do Christians believe about abortion?

There is no specific teaching in the Bible about abortion, so Christians have to use their understanding of Christian principles to help them decide how they should think and act. Many Christians believe that a baby has a **soul** from the moment it is **conceived** and is therefore fully human from that point, although often it is unclear what is meant by the soul. Both the Roman Catholic Church and the Church of England are opposed to abortion. The Roman Catholic Church does not permit abortion under any circumstances. The Church of England only approves abortion in exceptional circumstances, for example if it is necessary to save the mother's life or if the pregnancy is the result of rape. Some Christians take a more liberal view but think that abortion should always be a last resort and that the final decision must be made by the parents. Most Christians agree that abortion should not be seen as a form of contraception.

## Your lesson objectives

**In this lesson you will:**

- understand what abortion is

- explain and evaluate different views about abortion.

## Your key words

**conceived**

the moment when an egg is fertilised by a sperm producing a new life

**foetus**

a young animal in the egg or womb

**rape**

sex without consent

**soul**

the spiritual part of a human regarded as immortal

## Learning about religion

1  At what point do you think a foetus becomes a human being? Does this affect your view of abortion?

2  'So God created man in his own image, in the image of God he created him; male and female he created them' (Genesis 1:27).

a  What do you think Christians understand by being made 'in the image of God'?

b  How might the belief that humans are created in the image of God affect someone's views about abortion?

# 5.6 What is abortion?

## Bahá'í

Bahá'ís believe that all life is sacred. Abortion is only acceptable if it is to save the mother's life but not simply because a child is unwanted.

## Hinduism

Many Hindu texts condemn abortion, since Hindus believe that the self enters the body at conception. Abortion betrays the trust placed by the reincarnating soul in its future parents. However, abortion is increasingly practised by many Hindus.

## Islam

Islam teaches that only Allah can decide when someone will be born or die. Muslims believe the foetus is a human being therefore abortion is murder and is only allowed if the mother's life is at risk.

## Judaism

Judaism teaches that all life is a sacred gift from G-d and abortion goes against G-d's plan for every individual. It is only allowed if the mother's life is at risk and the decision must be made by the mother herself.

## Zoroastrianism

Zoroastrians believe human beings share the spiritual qualities of Ahura Mazda (God) and that they must keep his creation pure. To destroy an unborn foetus would interfere with the purity and order of his creation.

## Buddhism

Many Buddhists believe that any abortion breaks the First Precept because it harms the unborn foetus. Some Buddhists believe that sometimes continuing an unwanted pregnancy can cause even greater harm.

## Humanism

Humanist views about abortion are influenced by scientific evidence, likely results and the rights and wishes of everyone involved. Humanists look for the kindest solution or the one that would cause least harm.

## Jainism

*Ahimsa* (non-violence) is central to Jain beliefs. Jains believe that all life forms are sacred and have a soul. To destroy an unborn foetus would be to harm a living being and is not encouraged.

## Sikhism

Sikhs believe that abortion is the destruction of a sacred life and goes against the grace and will of God. Abortion is only acceptable if the mother's life is at risk or if the pregnancy is the result of rape.

# Drawing it all together

## Learning about religion

1 Explain the reasons why one or more of the religions you have studied are opposed to abortion.

2 For what reasons might some religious believers say that in certain circumstances abortion is acceptable?

## Learning from religion

1 What are the main differences between the Humanist view of abortion and religious views? Do you think it is easier to make decisions about questions of life and death, such as abortion, if you are religious? Give reasons and compare your view with others in your group.

**Hint** You need to think about the differences between following a rule laid down by a religion and making decision based on your own understanding of the issues involved.

2 Make a list of human qualities that could be described as spiritual.

**Hint** Being spiritual is not the same as being religious.

3 Write a list of all the positive aspects of having children and a list of any negative ones. Which is the longest list?

**Hint** You could compare your list with those of others in your group and discuss whether the good things you have listed outweigh the negative ones.

# 5.7 Ending a life

## Your lesson objectives

**In this lesson you will:**

- explain what is meant by euthanasia and suicide
- evaluate Christian responses to euthanasia and suicide.

## Do we have the right to die when we choose?

Most people agree that everyone has a right to live, but what happens when someone does not want to go on living?

Euthanasia, sometimes called 'mercy killing' or 'assisted suicide', means 'a good death'. It describes situations where the time and manner of death is chosen either by the person or by someone close to them if they are too ill to make the choice themselves. In the UK it is illegal to help someone end their life. **Suicide** is when someone decides to take their own life, perhaps because they are depressed and feel that life is not worth living.

## Your key words

**compassionate**
showing sympathy and care for others

**palliative care**
working to help ease the pain of someone who is dying

**secular**
having no spiritual or religious basis

**suicide**
killing yourself intentionally

**terminally ill**
suffering from a fatal disease

SAMARITANS CARE
TALK TO US ANYTIME
NIGHT OR DAY ON
0845 790 9090

This sign is on the Clifton Suspension Bridge in Bristol, UK. Many people have committed suicide here. Samaritans train volunteers to understand suicide and help people in distress.

# What do Christians believe about euthanasia and suicide?

Christians believe that life is sacred, that it was given by God and that only God can take it away. The sixth commandment forbids murder. Roman Catholics believe that suicide is a grave sin.

Although most Christians believe it is wrong to take your own life, they believe that God is forgiving and **compassionate** and that they have a responsibility to care for others in need. Many Christians work in hospices to care for people who are **terminally ill**, providing pain relief and **palliative care** to ensure that they suffer as little as possible in the period leading up to death. Roman Catholics have a special sacrament to prepare people for death.

Samaritans is an organisation which provides 24-hour telephone and online counselling for people who feel suicidal and need someone to talk to. It was set up in 1953 by Reverend Chad Varah, a Christian vicar, after he had conducted the funeral of a 13-year-old girl who had killed herself. Today Samaritans has 22,000 volunteers from all faiths and also **secular** backgrounds who help people who are in despair.

## Your discussion

Should people who are terminally ill be able to choose when they want to die? Should their close relatives and friends be allowed to help them?

## Learning about religion

1  Why do many Christians believe that euthanasia is wrong?

2  How might Christians try to help and support people who are dying or in distress?

3  Why do you think Chad Varah called his organisation 'Samaritans'?

# 5.7 Ending a life

## Bahá'í
Bahá'ís believe that they should be happy when someone dies because they are going on to the next world. They believe everyone is in the world for a reason so ending a life is not acceptable because it interferes with God's purpose.

## Hinduism
Hindus believe that ending life prematurely rarely helps the soul avoid the results of the *karma* it has accumulated. There are exceptions, such as when a terminally ill person is permitted to fast, even if this hastens death. In this case fasting is thought to clarify the consciousness.

## Islam
Islam teaches that only Allah can decide when someone will be born or die. Neither euthanasia nor suicide is acceptable because choosing to end life interferes with Allah's plan.

## Judaism
Judaism teaches that all life is sacred so suicide and euthanasia are unacceptable. Some Jews agree to withdrawal of life support if there is no hope of recovery.

## Zoroastrianism
Zoroastrians believe that during their lives on earth human souls can work towards becoming perfect beings of light. To interfere with that process would be against the will of God and is not acceptable.

## Buddhism
Many Buddhists believe that causing death breaks the First Precept because it harms the body. Some Buddhists believe that passive euthanasia, by withdrawing life support for example, is acceptable.

## Humanism
Humanists believe that everyone has the right to choose when they will die and that they should respect this decision in others. Humanists support a change in the law which would allow people to help someone to die.

## Jainism
Jains believe all life is sacred and that to end life would attract negative *karma*. Some Jains practise a holy fast when they are close to death, gradually ceasing to eat and drink. They hope for a calm and contented death with their mind focused on spiritual matters

## Sikhism
Sikhs believe that life is sacred and that only God can decide when it should come to an end. Euthanasia and suicide are against Sikh beliefs but Sikhs do not believe life should be artificially prolonged by life-support machines.

# Drawing it all together

## Learning about religion

**1** Explain why one or more of the religions you have studied are opposed to euthanasia under any circumstances.

**2** Explain why some religious people might view death as a happy, rather than a sad event.

## Learning from religion

**1** When, if ever, do you think euthanasia is acceptable? Explain your reasons.

**Hint** Remember there is a difference between voluntary euthanasia, which is when someone has expressed the wish to end their life, and involuntary euthanasia where the decision has been taken by others.

**2** 'Everyone has the right to choose when and how they will die.' Do you agree or disagree? What are the arguments for and against this point of view?

**Hint** When you have weighed up the arguments carefully you could organise a class debate on this topic.

**3** What is the difference between agreeing to the withdrawal of life support and helping someone to die?

**Hint** Some people who hold religious beliefs would consent to the withdrawal of life support but not agree with euthanasia.

# Your Assessment

What are the three most valuable rights and freedoms you enjoy in your life? How would your life be affected if they were taken away?

**Hint** Start by making a list of all the rights and freedoms you have and then put them in order of importance. Look at the teachings about rights and responsibilities you have learnt about to help you decide what matters most to you.

# 6 Religion in the world

## The bigger picture

In this chapter you will explore how the world is treated by humans. Damage to the world we live in – environmental damage – is often seen as one of the biggest threats to life today.

You will consider why religious believers claim the world is sacred and how they try to reduce the damage caused.

How can people tackle this problem in the modern world?

You will think about whether it is ever right to fight and look at the idea of war.

## Learning about religion

1 Make a list of all the wonderful things in the world and all the terrible things you see. Do you think the world is a good place to live?

2 Create an ideas map showing all the ways in which you think the world has been damaged. Colour code your ideas to show the ones which you believe may be reversible and those that are permanent. Share your thoughts with a partner.

### Your discussion

In pairs discuss the following statement: 'The biggest challenge facing the world today is environmental damage.' Make a list of ideas agreeing and disagreeing with this statement to feed back to your class.

# 6 Introduction What is happening to the environment?

## Your lesson objectives

**In this lesson you will:**

- identify ways in which the earth is being mistreated

- analyse why this is happening

- evaluate whether damaging the earth is a price worth paying for progress.

## Your key words

**atmosphere**

a layer of gases surrounding the earth

**developed world**

countries with high levels of national income, education, life expectancy and similar benefits

**developing world**

countries with lower levels than developed countries of benefits such as national income, education and life expectancy

**evidence**

facts that can be used as proof

## How is the earth being mistreated?

Scientists are able to provide plenty of **evidence** to show that human beings are damaging the earth. This damage is causing people in the **developing world** to die, because they are unable to cope with the effects of the actions of those in the **developed world**.

Most scientific evidence would suggest that the world is gradually heating up (**global warming**). This is causing the ice at both the North and South Poles to melt. The water produced from the melting of this ice can only go into the sea. As a result, sea levels are rising and some coastal areas are now at greater risk of flooding. Both the Netherlands and Bangladesh are low-lying countries. Being a developed country, the Netherlands can usually cope with any problems this may cause but in developing countries like Bangladesh rising sea levels have caused the flooding of large amounts of land that is used for growing crops. If crops fail, many people die of starvation because the country cannot afford to buy supplies from other countries. In some other developing countries, global warming has made it even more difficult to grow crops, especially as drought has become a bigger problem than ever before.

Most scientists believe that the reason the world is gradually heating up is because of the **greenhouse effect**.

The gases in the **atmosphere** trap some of the heat from the sun. This warms the earth, making it possible for life to exist here. However, burning fossil fuels such as coal and oil produces carbon dioxide in addition to other gases, and this means that more heat from the sun is trapped, making the earth warmer.

Since trees reduce the amount of carbon dioxide on earth while increasing the amount of oxygen, which is essential for life, you might assume they would be protected. However, large areas of forests are cut down and burnt every year in an attempt to get more land to grow crops on. This produces more carbon dioxide, contributing further to the greenhouse effect , which in turn is contributing to the global warming that is threatening the planet.

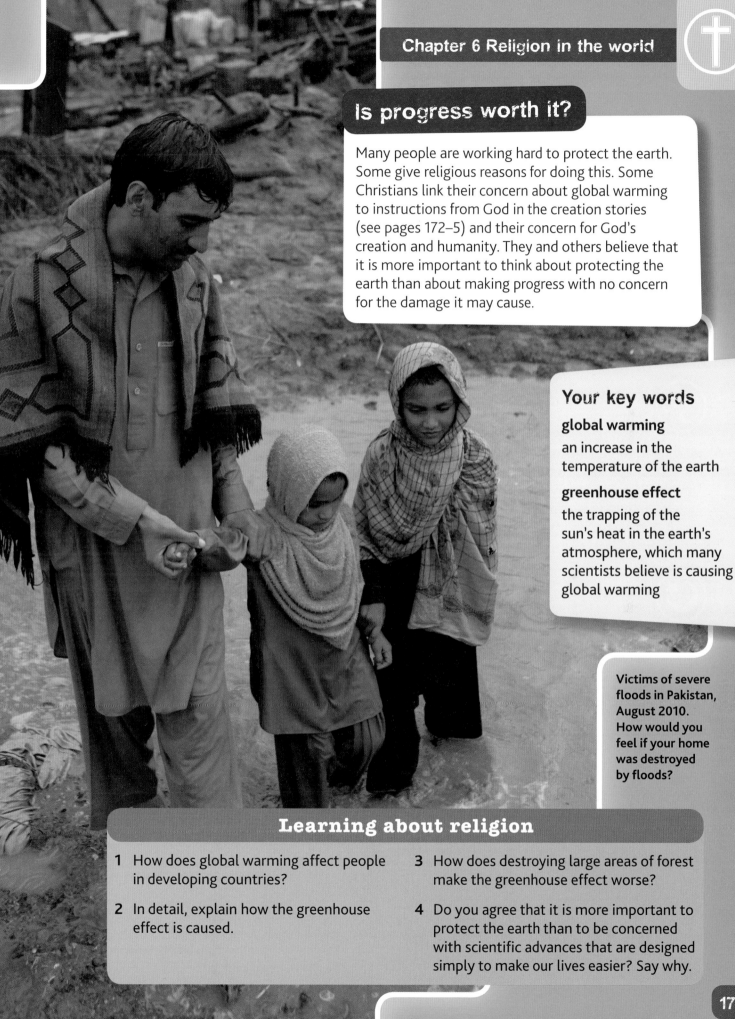

## Is progress worth it?

Many people are working hard to protect the earth. Some give religious reasons for doing this. Some Christians link their concern about global warming to instructions from God in the creation stories (see pages 172–5) and their concern for God's creation and humanity. They and others believe that it is more important to think about protecting the earth than about making progress with no concern for the damage it may cause.

### Your key words

**global warming**
an increase in the temperature of the earth

**greenhouse effect**
the trapping of the sun's heat in the earth's atmosphere, which many scientists believe is causing global warming

Victims of severe floods in Pakistan, August 2010. How would you feel if your home was destroyed by floods?

## Learning about religion

1 How does global warming affect people in developing countries?

2 In detail, explain how the greenhouse effect is caused.

3 How does destroying large areas of forest make the greenhouse effect worse?

4 Do you agree that it is more important to protect the earth than to be concerned with scientific advances that are designed simply to make our lives easier? Say why.

# 6 Introduction What is happening to the environment?

### Bahá'í

Bahá'ís work hard to protect the environment to keep it fit for future generations of people to live on. They see the divine in nature and therefore look after the earth, guided by the idea of the oneness of humanity.

### Hinduism

Many Hindu teachings indicate the need to protect the environment. Ideas relating to this include stewardship, global *karma*, the role of animals like the cow and bull, and the sanctity of rivers and mountains. Relevant values include *ahimsa* (non-violence), freedom from greed, and sustainability, linked to the god Vishnu.

### Islam

Muslims believe that they are *khalifah*s (stewards) with the responsibility to care for Allah's earth. Many of the things that are going wrong are the fault of humans, who are not exercising this responsibility properly.

### Judaism

Jews consider people to be stewards of G-d's earth. They have a responsibility to look after the environment for G-d and any problems the earth faces may well be the result of humans exercising their stewardship badly.

### Buddhism

Buddhism does not say how the earth came into being but Buddhists insist that for the sake of all living creatures on the earth, the environment should be looked after. Many things that are going wrong are due to human activity.

### Humanism

Most Humanists have a scientific view of the earth. They recognise that we all need the resources the earth provides for our survival so are keen to protect them.

### Jainism

Jains believe that all life is interdependent. There are five elements of nature that must be treated as living beings: land, water resources, fire, air and trees and plants. As these are all parts of the environment, it should be cared for.

### Sikhism

Sikhs believe the earth exists because God wants it to exist. Out of respect for God, the earth has to be respected. Damaging the environment is disrespectful to God.

### Zoroastrianism

Zoroastrianism has always been concerned about improving the quality of life on the earth. They believe that over the years humans have disregarded the effects that their actions have had on the environment and this must be corrected.

# Drawing it all together

## Learning about religion

1 Make a list of things that you think are going wrong with the environment. Compare your list with a partner.

2 Why do believers of the religions you have learnt about think the environment should be protected?

## Learning from religion

1 Explain the link between religion and the environment.

**Hint** Consider the religious beliefs you have learnt about.

2 You have been asked to speak to a meeting of people from several different religions. Your task is to persuade them that people need to do more to protect the environment. Working with a partner, create a presentation to explain your ideas.

**Hint** You need to think about religious teachings as well as scientific ideas.

3 'Science provides people with an explanation of the causes of environmental problems.'

'Religion provides people with a feeling of awe and wonder at the way God has created such beauty.'

Do you agree with these statements? Say why/why not.

**Hint** Think about each view before deciding.

# 6.1 Use it or abuse it?

## Your lesson objectives

**In this lesson you will:**

- identify Christian beliefs about the environment and how the planet should be treated

- reflect on why environmental damage is an important issue for Christians

- evaluate whether it is right for the world to be protected even if this means hardship for humans.

## Your key words

**belief**

accepting that something is true or real

**Bible**

a word used for the sacred writings of the Jews (Tenakh) and Christians (Old and New Testaments)

**dominion**

being in charge of, or having power over, something

**environment**

surroundings

**stewardship**

looking after something for someone else

## What do Christians believe about the world?

Christians believe that God created the world and that it is very special. They think that God gave humans a particular responsibility to care for and look after the world. This is an idea known as **stewardship**.

However, Christians also believe that they have **dominion** over the world. This means they are in control of it for God. The idea that they are in control may lead to some people in the world thinking they can use what the earth provides without any thought for the results. Christians, however, say that the earth belongs to God and that they are his stewards.

## How do Christians believe they should treat the world?

Christians do not believe that the world is theirs to keep, or to abuse. The **Bible** teaches that it is a special gift entrusted to them by God which they should look after:

> God blessed them and said to them, 'Be fruitful and increase in number; fill the earth and subdue it. Rule over the fish of the sea and the birds of the air and over every living creature that moves on the ground.'
>
> (Genesis 1:28)

> The LORD God took the man and put him in the Garden of Eden to work it and take care of it.
>
> (Genesis 2:15)

As a result of this **belief**, many Christians are trying to be more involved in caring for the **enviroment** and show their support for reducing the harm caused to the planet in order to preserve it for future generations.

The Garden of Eden, painted on a tiled floor in the church of St Michele Arcangelo, Anacapri, Capri, Italy.

The picture on the left, of a rubbish tip, shows one aspect of how the world is being damaged. What is your reaction to this?

## Learning about religion

1 Explain in your own words what the quotes from Genesis are saying about how people should treat the environment.

2 Explain why Christians believe caring for the environment is so important.

3 Read the passage below about Christopher Columbus exploring the Haitian island of La Gonâve.

### The island of La Gonâve

Over 500 years ago, Christopher Columbus wrote about the forests on the Haitian island of La Gonâve. He described the trees as 'so tall, they seemed to be scratching heaven'. Today, the land where they stood is empty. When it rains, the top layer of soil erodes away, causing floods. Many people have died and buildings have been destroyed or damaged. Floods are natural disasters but perhaps they happen partly due to the people not caring for the land. They cut down trees to make charcoal to sell or cook with. It is their only method of survival. However, without the trees, the land is not protected and when the floods come, the soil is washed away and flooding occurs.

a What causes the flooding on the island of La Gonâve?

b What do you think a Christian might say about the behaviour described above?

c Are the people fulfilling the responsibility of caring for God's planet? What is your view?

# 6.1 Use it or abuse it?

## Bahá'í
Bahá'ís believe that everything we see in the world around us is intended to show people how wonderful God is. Because of this people have a duty to protect nature and the environment.

## Buddhism
For Buddhists, everything is connected – humans, animals and plants. They believe in acting wisely in the world just as the Buddha did in his many lives.

## Hinduism
Hindus believe they should be thankful for nature and the environment. They believe that they should protect and not damage them.

## Humanism
Many Humanists believe that they must work to take care of the environment for the sake of the future of human beings and of animals.

## Jainism
Jains believe they should try to do the least amount of harm possible, in order to preserve the world.

## Islam
Islam teaches that Allah created the whole world as a place of worship and that anyone who plants a tree and cares for it is looking after the world and will be rewarded.

## Sikhism
Sikhs believe that everything we see in the world was designed and created by God. Sikhs are asked to respect this world in order to show respect to its creator.

## Judaism
Judaism teaches that caring for the environment is important, as it is G-d's creation and humans have a duty to look after it. This is known as 'stewardship'.

## Zoroastrianism
Zoroastrians believe that Ahura Mazda created the world through his action and it is important that humans also act in the world.

# Drawing it all together

## Learning about religion

1 Take two of the religions you have learnt about. Make a list for each of them showing what they believe about caring for the world.

2 Write a definition of these words:

entrusted

steward.

## Learning from religion

1 Write down the ways in which you are active in the world – do you think that you make a difference? For example, have you taken part in a litter pick; do you recycle as much as you can?

**Hint** Make sure that you answer the question honestly and think about both practical activities and any campaigning for change that you do.

2 Create two lists of the ways in which the environment has been damaged. In one list, you should put damage caused by people and in the other list, damage which you think might be due to natural causes.

**Hint** Remember that some natural disasters may be caused by humans.

3 Do you think that if you believed in a future life on earth it would affect how you treat the environment? Try to give some examples from the religions you have studied.

**Hint** In your answer you need to think about a religion which believes in reincarnation as well as about Christianity.

# 6.2 Is the earth sacred?

## Your lesson objectives

**In this lesson you will:**

- understand the meaning of the word 'sacred'

- understand why Christians believe the earth is sacred

- analyse Christian claims that the earth is sacred.

## What does being sacred mean?

The word '**sacred**' has several meanings. A simple meaning is 'connected with religion'. More usefully, something that is sacred is 'considered to be special and holy'.

## Your key words

**sacred**
considered to be special and holy

William Blake, *The Ancient of Days*, wood engraving, c.1790. How does the image show the power of God in creating the world?

178

## Learning about religion

1  Explain what the word 'sacred' means.

2  Give a summary of the Genesis creation story. You can read it in the Bible (Genesis 1:1–2:3).

3  Explain why Christians believe the earth is sacred.

## Why do Christians believe the earth is sacred?

The Bible opens with a story describing how God created the earth in six days: 'In the beginning God created the heavens and the earth' (Genesis 1:1). It does not explain how the earth was created, but it then goes on to recount how the earth was made ready for creatures to live on.

Light, the sky, land, plants and then other planets were made by the end of the fourth day. On the fifth day, creatures that live in the sea and the air were created. On the sixth day, land animals and humans were created. The story tells us that having been blessed by God, humans were made stewards of the earth.

On the seventh day of creation, God rested and blessed the seventh day (Saturday) as a special day. This is why Jews observe the Sabbath on Saturday. Christians have made their special day Sunday instead, to recognise the importance of Jesus rising from the dead on what has become Easter Sunday.

However, having created the earth and all the life on earth, God did not abandon his creation. The second creation story is followed by the story of Adam and Eve disobeying God by eating the fruit of the Tree of the Knowledge of Good and Evil in the Garden of Eden. As a result, they became aware that they were naked and tried to clothe themselves with leaves. The story makes it quite clear that God is going to be involved with his creation. Even after Adam and Eve had disobeyed him and were facing punishment, he was prepared to help them: 'The LORD God made garments of skin for Adam and his wife and clothed them' (Genesis 3:21).

## Is the earth sacred?

The answer to this question seems to depend on whether a person believes that God had a role in creation. If he did, then using the simple definition of sacred, 'connected with religion', it is easy to argue that the earth is sacred. Christians believe that because the earth is sacred and belongs to God, humans have the responsibility of looking after it for him. This includes everything that lives on the planet.

### Your discussion

Do you agree that the earth is sacred?

What are the arguments for and against this idea?

# 6.2 Is the earth sacred?

### Bahá'í
There is a strong belief in the Bahá'í Faith that God is the creator of the universe but it is not important to know how he created it. What is important is that every person is a child of God and should be treated with great respect.

### Hinduism
Hindus believe that everything in the universe originated from the Supreme. The earth is considered to be a goddess and part of a Hindu's *dharma* (duty) is to look after all living creatures.

### Islam
The Qur'an has information about creation. Muslims believe that Allah created the earth and everything that exists on it. Humans must look after the earth for Allah.

### Judaism
Jews believe that G-d created the universe and that originally it was perfect. This makes it sacred, so humans must look after it for G-d and try to keep it as perfect as possible.

### Zoroastrianism
Zoroastrians believe that originally there was nothing in the world except the 'Wise Lord', Ahura Mazda, and the evil spirit, Angra Mainyu. Ahura Mazda created people to do good deeds to limit the evil of Angra Mainyu. As the earth is the creation of God, it is really sacred.

### Buddhism
Buddhists believe that the earth must be preserved and that no living thing must be harmed. Although they do not believe that any supreme god created the earth, humans have a responsibility to look after all species.

### Humanism
Humanists do not believe that the earth was made by any god, preferring to accept a more scientific explanation for its creation. The earth should be looked after, though, and this is a responsibility that all people share.

### Jainism
Jains believe that the earth is sacred and eternal – it has no beginning and will not end. It must be looked after as part of the Jain belief in not harming living things. There are 8,400,000 types of life and they are all interdependent.

### Sikhism
Although Sikhs do not have a creation story, they believe God had the leading role in the creation of the earth, so it is sacred. Humans must look after the earth as part of their *dharma* (duty).

# Drawing it all together

## Learning about religion

1 Take two of the religions you have learnt about. For each, write a sentence to explain how they think the earth came into being.

2 How does each of these religions expect people to treat the earth?

## Learning from religion

1 Does it matter whether God made the earth or not? Why?

**Hint** Think about reasons for looking after the earth.

2 Do you think humans have abused the responsibility God gave them for planet earth? In what ways is this seen in the world today?

**Hint** Make sure you have thought about the reasons for your opinion before you write your answer.

3 Do you think the earth will ever be perfect? Discuss this question in pairs and be prepared to share your opinions with the class.

**Hint** Many religions believe that the earth was perfect when God created it.

# 6.3 What can we do?

## Your lesson objectives

**In this lesson you will:**

- understand ways in which people are working to improve the environment

- understand why Christians believe they should work to improve the environment.

## Your key words

**community**

a group of people who share something in common

**greenhouse gases**

gases that contribute to the greenhouse effect, for example methane and carbon dioxide

**landfill site**

a place where large quantities of rubbish are buried

**Salvation Army**

a Christian organisation actively working within the community

## What are people doing to improve the environment?

It is easy to use the excuse that anything an individual does to help the environment will make little difference because the problem is too big for one person to solve. Christians would not accept this view. While they acknowledge that one person cannot achieve much alone, they realise that millions of people can make a difference. One person changing to driving a car with low carbon dioxide emissions will not help much, but a million people doing so will help significantly to reduce the amount of carbon dioxide released into the atmosphere, thereby contributing less to the greenhouse effect.

There is an important movement in the Anglican Church towards green issues including using solar panels on churches. The **Salvation Army**, a Christian organisation, collects clothing that people no longer want. Instead of throwing it into a **landfill site**, where it will produce **greenhouse gases** as it breaks down, the Salvation Army recycles it. It does this by selling the clothing at low prices in charity shops or by giving it to the homeless and others who are in need. All money collected is spent on helping the poorest members of the **community**.

It has been estimated that 800 litres of water are needed to make a t-shirt, and that when a person has finished with an article of clothing it still has 70 per cent of its useful life left. So clothes recycling not only saves useful garments from being thrown away, it also helps to save valuable resources.

**Clothes being sorted for recycling, Salvation Army Trading Company, Northamptonshire, UK, 2005. In what ways does this help poorer people?**

## Why do Christians believe they should help to improve the environment?

If life on earth ends in 100 years because of the way we have treated the planet, it will probably not have a direct effect on any of us. However, it may have a devastating effect on our children and grandchildren. No one can say with any certainty that our actions will destroy the earth, but just because we probably will not be here to see it does not mean that it will not happen.

For Christians there is another reason why they should look after the earth. They believe that it belongs to God and not to us, so we are destroying something that is not ours to destroy. A Christian's relationship with planet earth should be judged by the Golden Rule – 'Treat others as you would wish to be treated'.

### Learning about religion

1   Explain why it is important that large numbers of people are involved in looking after the earth.

2   Explain how the Salvation Army is helping to look after the earth and the people living on it.

3   Why does helping the environment matter to Christians? Give two reasons.

# 6.3 What can we do?

## Bahá'í

In 2009, representatives of the Bahá'í Faith decided to use a system of training institutes to encourage members of the Bahá'í community to take part in voluntary work related to environmental sustainability.

## Buddhism

The Buddhist Dharma Gaia Trust was set up to make people more aware of Buddhism and ecology by helping people to work on environmental projects such as the 'Temple Forest Project' in Sri Lanka.

## Hinduism

Hindu Seva Pratishthna has set up a project in India to educate farmers on environment-friendly methods of farming and offers assistance in using these methods.

## Humanism

Many Humanist groups in the UK support local and international environmental projects to improve the lives of people.

## Islam

Muslims have established Muslim Associations for Climate Change Action (MACCA), to encourage among other things a 'Green *Hajj*', with the idea that by 2018 the traditional Islamic pilgrimage will be recognised as environmentally friendly.

## Jainism

Jains are always willing to look positively and with enthusiasm on environmental causes. In India and abroad, they help to bring greater awareness and put into practice their principles on ecology, welfare of the poor and the aged and animals, using volunteers to help.

## Judaism

The Big Green Jewish campaign has been set up to help Jews to work toward a better future, with a healthy environment, 'green' jobs and a secure energy future.

## Sikhism

Many *gurdwaras* encourage Sikhs to recycle, reuse, compost their waste, use 'green' energy and harvest rainwater in order to look after the earth and its resources.

## Zoroastrianism

Zoroastrianism encourages believers to care for the earth and all life after 'the earth'. For this reason they become involved in environmental projects across the world.

# Drawing it all together

## Learning about religion

1 Take two of the religions you have learnt about and say what each is doing to look after the earth.

2 Why do you think religious people get involved in looking after the earth?

## Learning from religion

1 'It is more important to teach others to look after the earth than to spend time doing it yourself.' Discuss your ideas about this with a partner and list points on both sides of the argument.

**Hint** You might like to organise a class debate on this topic and try to reach a conclusion.

2 Many people of faith believe that greed, hatred and stupidity are the reasons why people are damaging the earth. Do you agree? Say why.

**Hint** Look at some of the statements opposite before you write your answer.

3 Find an example of an environmental problem. What are religious people doing to help?

**Hint** Carry out some research into religious responses to environmental problems.

# 6.4 Is it ever right to fight?

## Your lesson objectives

**In this lesson you will:**

- increase your understanding of why people fight

- evaluate whether fighting is justified.

## Why do people fight?

People have fought for almost as long as humans have existed. In the Bible the first fight is between the brothers Cain and Abel in Genesis 4:1–8. People have given a lot of reasons for fighting, some better than others. Some Christians might say that fighting is one of the results of the Fall (see page 119). There are people who have gained a lot from fighting. However, such gains often come at a cost: even winners can get hurt and, of course, losers get hurt more.

Many people think that fighting is a natural reaction to certain circumstances. If people feel threatened, they can either fight or look for a different solution, such as running away. Psychologists call this 'fight or flight'.

Of course, a fight between two individuals does cause less damage than a fight between two countries (war). War has to be planned over a period of time to make sure the armed forces involved are prepared for what they have to do and have the money to pay for armaments and the people who fight in the armies. Wars can take many years to end once they have started. Millions may die.

Fights between two individuals may be unplanned and finish quickly when one person does not want to continue, or is unable to do so.

Some people think that fighting in self-defence is acceptable, although some try to find a peaceful solution. They say that it takes a stronger person to decide not to fight than to fight – which they may see as the easy way out.

**What do you think is worth fighting for?**

## Learning about religion

1 Explain fully why some people fight.

2 Why did many Christians decide that it was right to fight in the Second World War?

## Can Christians justify fighting?

Christian leaders have always had to decide whether or not to support wars. On many occasions, they have decided that war is the best option. A good example of this is the Second World War (1939–45), when leaders felt that fighting the threat of a Nazi invasion of the UK was the only option open to them and that nothing else would work. Few Christians disagreed and many fought bravely for their country.

However, support for some other wars has not been so clear cut. In 2003, the UK joined a war in Iraq because it was believed that Iraq possessed and would have used weapons of mass destruction. Many Christians were not convinced that this was right. As it turned out, there were no such weapons. Christians would also refer to examples from Jesus' life and teachings such as in Matthew 21:12 (when he threw the money-changers and dove-sellers out of the Temple) and Matthew 26:52 (when he said that people who lived by the sword would die by the sword).

# 6.4 Is it ever right to fight?

## Bahá'í
As Bahá'ís believe in the equality of all humans, they think that all people should live in peace. They see world peace as the next stage in the evolution of the planet and work towards establishing it.

## Buddhism
Buddhists believe in *metta/maitri* (loving kindness) and this makes fighting difficult to justify. Buddhists concentrate on living in a way that does not mean that others want to fight them.

## Hinduism
In the traditional *varna* system, the kshatriya (warrior) class were allowed to use violence to protect the innocent and maintain peace and order. However, the general principle followed by Hindus is to practise *ahimsa* (non-violence).

## Humanism
Humanists believe that, as human life is precious, war is wrong. It ruins lives, wastes resources and damages the environment. It must be a last resort.

## Islam
Muslims will fight to defend their nation and their religion (lesser *jihad*) but the internal struggle to do good and live as Allah wants them to (greater *jihad*) is more important.

## Jainism
Jains believe in *ahimsa* – the principle of non-violence. Harming any living thing not only harms the individual but also harms their journey to liberation. Therefore most Jains will not fight although self-defence is acceptable.

## Judaism
Although Jews fought many wars on G-d's instruction in the times of the Jewish scriptures, nowadays they see peace as something to work towards and peaceful methods should be used before fighting takes place.

## Sikhism
Sikhs believe that God wants them to promote human rights and to live in harmony. If this has to be brought about by fighting, Sikhs will fight, but only if there is no alternative.

## Zoroastrianism
Zoroastrians believe that war is the result of evil forces that tempt humans into making bad decisions. It should, therefore, be avoided if possible but Zoroastrianisns have to fight all evil and this can include humans.

# Drawing it all together

## Learning about religion

1 How do the religions you have learnt about respond to the question 'Is it ever right to fight?' Are there differences in the reasons given for their responses?

2 Do you think a religious person would be more prepared to fight for their nation or for their religion? Explain why.

## Learning from religion

1 Do you think it is ever right to fight? If so, explain under what circumstances, if not, explain why not.

**Hint** When making your decision, choose the response for which you feel there are the stronger reasons.

2 'It is kinder and more loving to fight than to refuse to fight.' What do you think?

**Hint** Think about what life might be like once a war has ended.

3 Is fighting a natural reaction for humans? Say why.

**Hint** Think about yourself and people you know to help you decide.

# 6.5 War and peace

## Your lesson objectives

**In this lesson you will:**

- understand how some Christians decide whether it is right to fight a war

- evaluate the merits of the Just War theory.

## How do Christians decide to fight?

Christians may not agree with fighting in a war. Some Christians, such as **Quakers**, are **pacifists** and will never take part in a war, whereas others may think carefully, take advice and pray before they make a decision that could end their own life or someone else's.

## Your key words

**civilian**

someone who is not a member of the armed forces

**just cause**

a reason that is morally right

**Just War theory**

a set of conditions first put forward by St Thomas Aquinas to decide whether it is right to fight a war

**opinion**

someone's personal view on a subject

**pacifist**

someone who believes that war is wrong

## Just War theory

**Just War theory** is based on whether it is just or fair to fight a war. It was first put forward by St Thomas Aquinas (1225–74), who was a great Christian thinker. Although it has changed a little over the years, it is still much the same as when Aquinas first suggested it. He said that in his **opinion**, Christians should fight in a war only if it was a Just War. He believed that a Just War had three conditions, all of which had to be met.

1 War must be declared by the countries' heads of state and not by military leaders.

2 There must be a **just cause**. This may be self-defence or fighting a tyrant who is taking away people's **rights** and freedoms.

3 The intention must be to advance what is good and not to promote evil.

Since then, other conditions have been added.

4 The amount of violence used must be controlled and be only enough to achieve the goal. **Civilians** should be protected.

5 There must be a good chance of success. Fighting a lost cause is a waste of life.

6 All other ways of resolving the dispute must have been tried before war can take place.

The principles of St Thomas Aquinas are still widely used by politicians and individuals, whether Christians or not, to decide whether it is right to fight. These principles have also been raised in the UK Parliament in connection with recent wars that the UK has been involved in.

British Paratroopers in Kandahar Province, Afghanistan in 2008. Many Christians are pacifists but others believe that it is their duty to fight if a war is declared by their country.

## Learning about religion

1 Pick out a key word or phrase from each of the six conditions of a Just War. Use them to make a spider diagram. For each one, draw a symbol to represent your chosen word or phrase.

2 Would the Just War conditions persuade you that it is right to fight? Explain why.

3 Which two conditions do you think a Christian would say are the most important?

### Your key words

**Quaker**
a member of the Christian denomination otherwise known as the Religious Society of Friends

**right**
the moral or legal claim to have or do something

### Your discussion

'If your country needs you to fight a war, no thought, discussion or prayer is required, you should just do it.'

Do you agree? Explain your answer.

# 6.5 War and peace

## Bahá'í

Bahá'u'lláh said that his followers should not fight to protect or promote the faith. Bahá'u'lláh taught that it is better to be killed than to kill.

## Buddhism

Although most Buddhists refuse to fight, they will stand up against threats to justice and human rights. This includes the right to practise religion freely.

## Hinduism

For Hindus, a peaceful society in impossible without inner peace and without freedom from greed, lust and anger. For maintaining order, the warrior class were allowed to fight according to their codes of bravery and courtesy.

## Humanism

Although Humanists believe every effort should be made to resolve conflicts peacefully, many believe that if war is in self-defence or in defence of the rights of others it can be justified.

## Islam

The idea of lesser *jihad* (holy war) allows Muslims to fight under certain strict conditions. These are designed to protect the innocent and prevent war being used to take another country's land or possessions.

## Jainism

Although self-defence is acceptable, many Jains believe it is never right to fight and will give up their lives rather than fight. Jains have never fought a war.

## Judaism

In the time of the Jewish scriptures, G-d sometimes commanded the Jewish people to fight. These were occasions such as where the Jews were trying to maintain their religion when other people wanted to make them worship false gods.

## Sikhism

Sikhs will fight a righteous war (*Dharam Yudh*) provided it is the last resort, is for a good reason such as defending their nation or faith and uses minimum force to achieve victory. All soldiers should be committed Sikhs.

## Zoroastrianism

Zoroastrians believe that most people fight because they are using their free will incorrectly. This keeps them from God. Restoring peace and preventing conflict as well as fighting eveil is the correct use of free will.

# Drawing it all together

## Learning about religion

1 Under what circumstances (if any) will followers of the religions you have learnt about decide it is right to fight? What are the differences in these circumstances between the religions?

2 Do you think good can come out of war? Explain your answer.

## Learning from religion

1 Is a peaceful world an ideal world? Say why.

**Hint** Think about the alternatives before deciding.

2 Should self-defence be the only reason for fighting? Explain why.

**Hint** Think about other reasons before deciding.

3 'Humans killing humans is always wrong.' Explain your thoughts about this statement.

**Hint** Try to decide whether there is ever a good reason for one human to kill another.

# 6.6 Say 'No' to war

## Your lesson objectives

**In this lesson you will:**

- investigate pacifism as an alternative to fighting
- evaluate whether pacifism is a valid response to a threat of violence.

## Your key words

**authority**

the power or right to be a leader of others

**conscience**

a knowledge of right and wrong which helps people make decisions

**conscientious objector**

a person who refuses to fight in a war because of their beliefs

**denomination**

a branch of a religion

**pacifism**

using peaceful methods to achieve an aim

**priest**

a person with the authority to perform religious ceremonies

## Pacifism – an alternative to fighting

Most Christian **denominations** offer their support to war if the reasons for going to war meet the conditions laid down in Just War theory. Military regiments have their own **priests** who offer support to soldiers and their families. Prayers are offered for those who will suffer on both sides and to ask that justice will be achieved. Some churches and cathedrals are directly associated with local regiments. However, some Christians feel uneasy about this. One denomination that stands out against violence of any sort is the Religious Society of Friends (Quakers).

In 1660, the Quakers gave a statement to King Charles II, which said: 'We utterly deny all outward wars and strife and fightings with outward weapons, for any end or under any pretence whatsoever, and this is our testimony to the whole world.'

Quakers believe not only that fighting in wars is wrong, but also that any form of violence is wrong. This is called **pacifism**. They are committed to the creation of a world where there is no violence between countries, between people or even within an individual. Quaker views on other topics reflect the desire to prevent conflict and bring about universal peace. They take their **authority** from teachings in the Bible such as 'You shall not murder' (Exodus 20:13) and 'Love your enemies and pray for those who persecute you' (Matthew 5:44b).

Quakers have been accused by some people of cowardice and giving in to aggression. They deny this and often refer to themselves as **conscientious objectors**. This means that they have an objection to fighting based on their **conscience**, which tells them that it is wrong to fight. During the Second World War, there were around 59,000 conscientious objectors in the UK. Not all of them were Quakers and many were Humanists. Many faced anger or were mocked for refusing to fight.

A dove bearing an olive branch is a symbol of pacifism following the story of the flood in Genesis 8.

## Is pacifism a valid alternative?

In order to show their opposition to Hitler's armies, during the Second World War many Quakers worked to support the war effort. They volunteered to help care for wounded soldiers, they carried stretchers and drove ambulances. These were all highly dangerous activities demanding courage, but Quakers were prepared to do them because they did not involve harming anybody.

Of course, if everyone was a pacifist, there would be no war or violence. Although this is an ideal that is unlikely ever to happen, Quakers, some other Christians and Humanists continue to work towards it.

## Learning about religion

1. Explain what you understand by the statement given to King Charles II in 1660.

2. Explain carefully the difference between a pacifist and a conscientious objector.

3. Do you think it was right for conscientious objectors in the Second World War to face anger and mockery? Say why, or why not.

4. Are Quakers wasting their time working towards peace throughout the world? Say why, or why not.

# 6.6 Say 'No' to war

## Bahá'í
Since 2004, many Bahá'ís have been arrested and imprisoned in Iran despite having committed no crime. Whilst the Bahá'í community is concerned about this, they have tried to raise awareness of this persecution across the world rather than using violent protest.

## Hinduism
The most famous Hindu pacifist was Mohandas Gandhi. In the early twentieth century, he organised strictly peaceful protests against British rule, increasing urbanisation and the economic exploitation of India.

## Islam
Islam means submission, obedience and surrender to the will of God. It is the name given to the religion revealed to the Prophet Muhammad ﷺ. It is through submission to the will of Allah that Muslims attain peace. Muslims wish to emphasise this idea to make war less likely.

## Judaism
Although there is little teaching about refusing to fight in the Tenakh, the prophet Isaiah looked forward to a time of peace and nowadays many Jews question whether it is right to fight.

## Buddhism
Buddhists are pacifists and would object to serving in the military because they do not believe in killing. To fight in a war would violate everything they believe in.

## Humanism
Bertrand Russell was a famous Humanist pacifist. He was sent to prison for opposing the First World War and in his later life campaigned strongly against nuclear weapons.

## Jainism
Jains believe that compassion for life is a vital principle. They believe that they should stand up for what is right but only fight in self-defence and as a last resort.

## Sikhism
Guru Nanak Dev Ji recognised peace as an ideal but some later *gurus* realised that if they were to survive Sikhs had to use force against their enemies. Nowadays, though, Sikhism does promote a non-violent approach to life.

## Zoroastrianism
Zoroastrians believe fighting is sometimes necessary to overcome evil people. They have a duty to oppose all evil.

# Drawing it all together

## Learning about religion

**1** Explain what the religions you have learnt about teach about saying 'No' to war.

**2** Explain why sometimes religious people may feel that it is necessary to fight.

## Learning from religion

**1** How do you think religious believers should respond to attacks on their religion? Explain why.

**Hint** You need to consider what other beliefs may be affected by their response.

**2** It takes a stronger person to refuse to fight than it does to fight. What do you think?

**Hint** Think about different types of strength and what some people think about people who refuse to fight.

**3** 'Religious people should not play video games about war.' Do you agree? Say why.

**Hint** Think about whether there is a difference between what is real and what is made up.

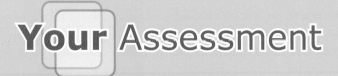

# Your Assessment

'We should spend more time looking after the earth and less time fighting wars.' How far do you agree with this statement? Give reasons to support your opinion.

How far would a religious believer agree with you?

**Hint** You should consider the religious teachings you have learnt about. Many of them apply to both the environment and war.

#  Religion and science

The Large Hadron Collider in Geneva, Switzerland is the biggest machine ever built by humans. It was designed to discover more about how the world began.

## The bigger picture

Science aims to explore and uncover how the world around us works. Many scientists would describe themselves as committed to this process. As they find out more and more about the world, scientists are discovering just how complex it is. For many scientists, this leads to a greater sense of respect for the process of creation and also a sense of wonder at just how this was possible. Many people of faith share this sense of respect and wonder.

This chapter will look at the relationship between religion and science. To begin, you will consider how the words 'proof' and 'truth' are used in the wider world, but also by scientists and religious believers. You will then explore the idea that it is possible to combine scientific ideas with religious belief. Later in the chapter you will examine two areas of scientific investigation that religions are concerned about.

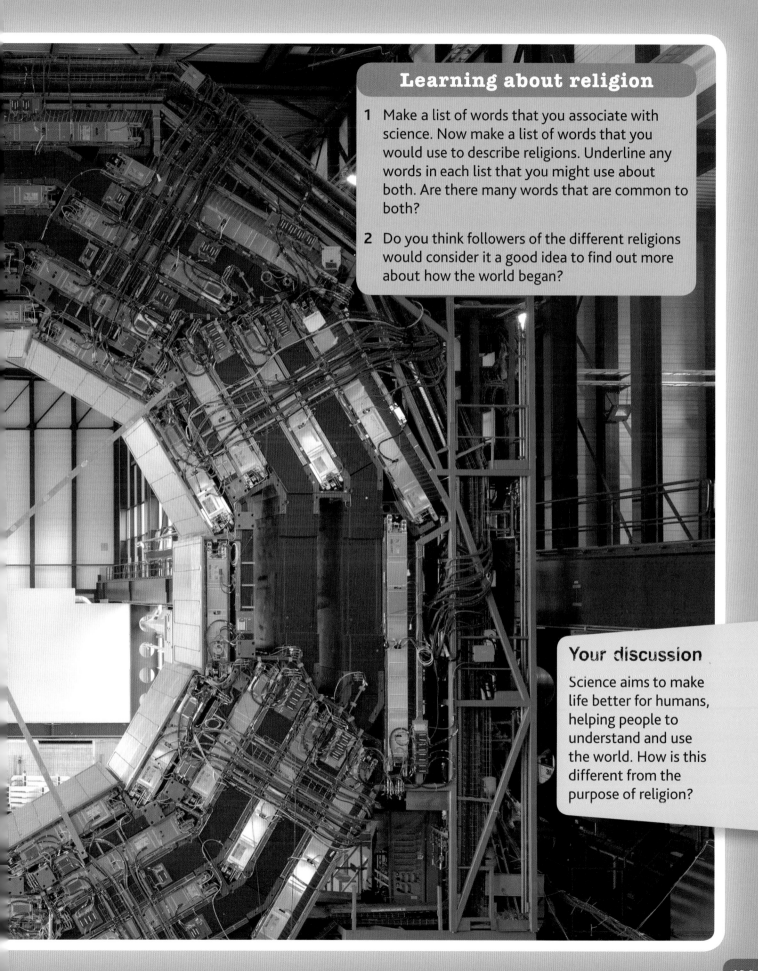

## Learning about religion

1. Make a list of words that you associate with science. Now make a list of words that you would use to describe religions. Underline any words in each list that you might use about both. Are there many words that are common to both?

2. Do you think followers of the different religions would consider it a good idea to find out more about how the world began?

### Your discussion

Science aims to make life better for humans, helping people to understand and use the world. How is this different from the purpose of religion?

# 7 Introduction

# How can we prove it?

## Your lesson objectives

In this lesson you will:

- consider how people gain knowledge of the world
- define the terms 'fact' and 'proof'
- identify the difference between facts and beliefs.

## Your key words

**evidence**
facts that can be used as proof

**fact**
something that can be proved to be true

**penicillin**
a medicine that is used to fight infection

**proof**
evidence that something is true or exists

## What can we know about the world?

Humans learn about the world using their senses. A child explores something new by using their hands to feel it and using their mouth to taste it. At school, learning takes place by listening in class or by looking at something. In a restaurant, the smell of food cooking may entice people to order something they have never tried before from the menu. Daily life is full of learning experiences that help people to gain knowledge of the world.

People's knowledge of the world helps them to make decisions, for example to decide what to eat for lunch, based on whether the food tastes nice. Everyone has senses, but not everyone's sense experiences are the same. For instance, someone who is short-sighted will not see the same view as someone with perfect vision. What smells good to one person may smell terrible to another. Our senses are not reliable in this way.

Scientists try to gather information that is reliable. To do this, they perform experiments and repeat them. By repeating experiments, scientists gain **evidence** that can be checked. When a piece of information has been checked and has been agreed on, it is called a '**fact**'. A fact is said to have been proved. This means that there is scientific evidence to say that it is true. The evidence is what people call '**proof**'.

Scientists spend their working lives investigating the world to establish facts. Facts help people to understand the world, and often support breakthroughs that improve life. For example, the discovery of **penicillin** has improved the health of millions of people.

## Can everything be checked to establish facts?

Sometimes it is not possible to check whether something is a fact. One example of this is ghosts. Some people claim to have seen them but so far their existence has not been proven. People might believe in ghosts but there is certainly no scientific proof that they exist.

Do we all experience different tastes in the same way?

### Learning about religion

1 Can you think of other examples of things that people believe in that cannot be proved or established as scientific fact?

2 Explain the difference between facts and beliefs in your own words, using your own examples.

# How can we prove it?

**Bahá'í**
For Bahá'ís proof is found through truth which they discover as they become closer to God through the way they live their lives.

**Buddhism**
Buddhism teaches that truth is found by achieving enlightenment. Truth then does not need proof. Scientific proof does not conflict with religious truth.

**Hinduism**
Hinduism accepts scientific proof provided it agrees with the teachings of the scriptures. Hindus believe that without personal character and insight, human views, analysis and evaluation are likely to lead to error and cheating.

**Humanism**
Humanists rely on human intelligence and reason and accept scientific proofs.

**Jainism**
Jains welcome scientific proofs as ways of helping them to understand the world. Jains believe that much of their religion has a scientific basis.

**Islam**
For Muslims truth is found in Islam as 'submission to the will of Allah'. However, they believe that science can help to explain things as humans develop and accept scientific proofs.

**Judaism**
Judaism teaches that truth is found in the Torah, which is the word of G-d. However, it is open to interpretation and most scientific claims can be accepted.

**Sikhism**
Sikhism accepts scientific truth provided that it does not go against fundamental religious teachings.

**Zoroastrianism**
Zoroastrians welcome scientific discoveries that can help improve the world.

# Drawing it all together

## Learning about religion

1 Looking at two or more of the religions you have studied, how do you think they would they answer the question: 'How can we prove it?'

2 Write a paragraph explaining what 'scientific proof' means and then say what is the difference between this and 'religious belief'.

## Learning from religion

1 Make a list of 10 things which you believe to be true. Now explain what proof you have that they are in fact true.

**Hint** You may find that you do not have proof for some things which you believe are true. Explain why this is the case.

2 Working with a partner, create a spider diagram. In the middle put the word 'Proof'. On each 'leg' give a way in which something can be proved.

**Hint** In your answer you need to look at what you have learnt in this section as well as including your own ideas.

3 'Science tells us more about truth than religion does.' Discuss this with a partner and draw up a table with points for and against the argument.

**Hint** Remember to consider different religious and non-religious views.

# 7.1 Where do we find 'truth'?

## Your lesson objectives

**In this lesson you will:**

- identify what is meant by the word 'true'

- consider the reasons Christians would give for their beliefs.

## Your key words

**belief**

accepting that something is true or real

**Bible**

a word used for the sacred writings of the Jews (Tenakh) and Christians (Old and New Testaments)

**conscience**

a knowledge of right and wrong which helps people make decisions

**revelation**

something revealed that was previously hidden

**scriptures**

holy or sacred writings

## True or false?

When someone says that something is 'true', what do they mean? One person could claim that it is true that all the angles in a triangle add up to 180 degrees. This type of statement is quite easy to check. If it can be checked and agreed as a fact, then it could be said to be true. If not, it is said to be false.

What about beliefs? Is it possible to say that a **belief** is true or false? Christians would argue that what they believe is true – if someone holds a belief, then they must think this. Although it might not be possible to prove their beliefs to be true, they would still support their beliefs with evidence.

## Truth in Christianity

One key aspect of being a Christian is believing that God exists. For many people this belief is difficult to accept. Two key things that most Christians would use to support the ideas that God exists are the **Bible** and the Church.

## The Bible as truth

Most Christians would claim that the Bible is a source of truth. For Christians, the Bible provides information about God, about Jesus and about how to live their lives. The Bible is often called the 'Word of God'. Christians differ on whether they think that every word in the Bible actually came from God or whether they think that it was only inspired by God. They generally agree that the Bible contains truth, for example that unconditional love is better than selfishness. The Bible explores the idea of God on which Christian beliefs are based.

## Learning about religion

Create an ideas map showing as many reasons or pieces of evidence as you can to support the claim that Christianity is true.

## Church teachings as truth

For Christian believers, their Church's teachings, distributed in **scriptures** or through its leaders' voices and the witness of generations of believers, are the sources of truth.

There are many other reasons why a Christian might also follow the teachings of Christianity, for example:

• they had a religious upbringing and believe in what their parents believed

• they have had a religious experience, such as a miracle, take place in their lives, which has convinced them of the truth of Christianity

• their **conscience** (inner voice) tells them that the teachings are true.

These reasons provide just some of the answers that Christians would give in response to the question 'Why do you think that Christianity is true?'

Christians believe that there are two types of **revelation** that can help them understand God.

• General Revelation is available to everyone (such as the beauty of creation).

• Special Revelation is, in particular, found in the Bible.

The opening of the Gospel of Matthew in a Slavonic Bible. All churches contain a copy of the Bible. The Bible has been translated into over 2000 languages.

# 7.1 Where do we find 'truth'?

## Bahá'í
The Bahá'í Faith teaches that truth is found in the teachings of Bahá'u'lláh and by becoming closer to God.

## Hinduism
Hinduism is also called 'Sanatana Dharma'('Eternal Law' or 'Eternal Truth'). For Hindus universal truths are found in scripture and in the realisations of pure, enlightened souls.

## Islam
For Muslims, the messages of the prophets are the word of God and must not be changed. When a Muslim hears the words of the Qur'an in Arabic they know they are hearing the messages exactly as God intended and they can be sure that this is the truth.

## Judaism
The Torah is the most important book in Judaism. It is traditionally believed to have been dictated to Moses by G-d. This means that it is literally the word of G-d himself. For Orthodox Jews today, this means that it is the supreme source of truth.

## Buddhism
Understanding reality, and seeing the world as it really is, is a key goal of Buddhism. Buddhists call this understanding 'enlightenment'.

## Humanism
Humanists use reason and evidence to work out whether something is true or not. They weigh up the evidence and find ways to test it before reaching a conclusion.

## Jainism
Jains believe that truth is many-sided and can only be seen completely by those who are enlightened. The path to liberation is seen as the ultimate truth.

## Sikhism
Sikhism teaches that all the words of the human *gurus* contain the truth. This truth is now found in the holy book, the Guru Granth Sahib Ji.

## Zoroastrianism
The Avesta explains that Zoroaster was given his messages through visions of Ahura Mazda himself. These visions showed Zoroaster the truth about God and the world and he spread this message to his followers. The Gathas contain hymns written by Zoroaster.

# Drawing it all together

## Learning about religion

1 Looking at two or more of the religions you have studied, explain where they believe truth can be found.

2 What do people mean when they say that something is the 'word of God'.

## Learning from religion

1 Here are six ways in which some people believe they can find truth:

- authority
- conscience
- culture
- feelings
- peer group
- reason.

Find out what each of these means and write an explanation of why people might see them as a source of truth.

**Hint** Look up each word to check that you understand it and can explain it properly.

2 Discuss with a partner what you believe are good ways of finding the truth.

**Hint** Use what you have written in answer to the question above and add some more ideas.

3 'We should look for truth in our own knowledge and understanding, not in religion.' Discuss with a partner arguments for and against this statement.

**Hint** Remember to consider different religious views.

# 7.2 Did we evolve?

## Your lesson objectives

**In this lesson you will:**

- recognise that Christians have different views on evolution

- understand some of the reasons for different Christian views.

## Your key words

**ancestor**

an earlier member of a species that present-day examples are descended from

**community**

a group of people who share something in common

**fossil record**

examples of organisms that lived and died some time ago, preserved in rocks

**myth**

a story which is used to describe an important belief using language that is colourful or relates to the supernatural

**theory of evolution**

the idea that all species living today are the result of a process of development that began with simple life forms more than three billion years ago

## The theory of evolution

In the 1850s, Charles Darwin put forward the theory that all species on the earth were related to each other. Darwin recognised that there were many similarities between species, and therefore argued that they must all have come from the same original **ancestor**.

By looking at the **fossil record**, Darwin found examples of possible ancestors for the species that exist today; this provided evidence for his theory. The idea that all life forms have evolved from each other is now generally accepted by the scientific **community**. This is known as the **theory of evolution**.

Lemurs are an illustration of Darwin's idea of evolution. They only exist on the island of Madagascar and there are around 50 species, all of which are related to a common ancestor.

## Creation in the Bible

The Bible begins with the Book of Genesis, which describes the creation of the world. This was written thousands of years ago, and explains how God created the world. It begins: 'In the beginning God created the heavens and the earth' (Genesis 1:1).

This account of creation goes on to describe how the world was created in stages. God begins by creating light and darkness, then the sky is separated from the waters and the land. Next, plant life is created, followed by the stars and the seasons. All kinds of animals are produced and then finally God brings humans into being: 'So God created man, in his own image, in the image of God he created him; male and female he created them' (Genesis 1:27).

This account does not match the explanation that scientists give for the creation of plants, animals and humans. Does this mean that Christians do not believe in evolution?

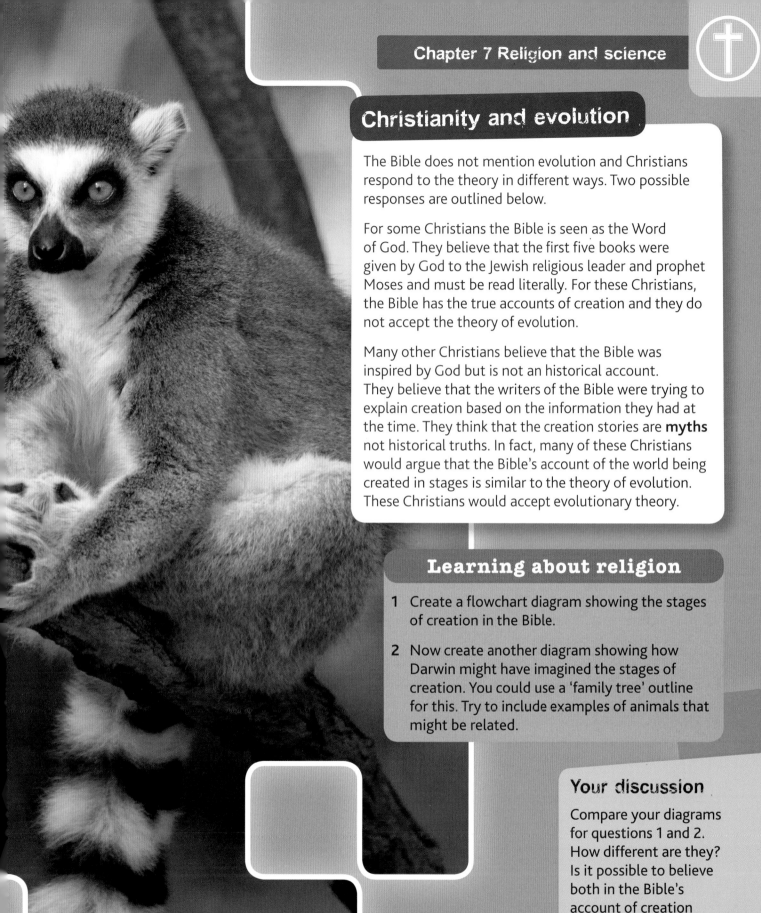

## Christianity and evolution

The Bible does not mention evolution and Christians respond to the theory in different ways. Two possible responses are outlined below.

For some Christians the Bible is seen as the Word of God. They believe that the first five books were given by God to the Jewish religious leader and prophet Moses and must be read literally. For these Christians, the Bible has the true accounts of creation and they do not accept the theory of evolution.

Many other Christians believe that the Bible was inspired by God but is not an historical account. They believe that the writers of the Bible were trying to explain creation based on the information they had at the time. They think that the creation stories are **myths** not historical truths. In fact, many of these Christians would argue that the Bible's account of the world being created in stages is similar to the theory of evolution. These Christians would accept evolutionary theory.

### Learning about religion

1 Create a flowchart diagram showing the stages of creation in the Bible.

2 Now create another diagram showing how Darwin might have imagined the stages of creation. You could use a 'family tree' outline for this. Try to include examples of animals that might be related.

### Your discussion

Compare your diagrams for questions 1 and 2. How different are they? Is it possible to believe both in the Bible's account of creation and in the theory of evolution?

# 7.2 Did we evolve?

### Bahá'í
The Bahá'í Faith tends to view the creation stories of other religions as religious myths and accepts scientific theories of evolution.

### Buddhism
Buddhist teachings focus on life now and how to escape the cycle of rebirth. Theories about how life evolved do not have any real effect on this.

### Hinduism
No account of creation in Hinduism mentions Darwinian evolution. Some teachings suggest a different form of evolution: that humans and lower species were created by gods and goddesses and humans are gradually evolving to become like them.

### Humanism
Humanists think science provides the only reliable source of knowledge about the universe and the origins of life on earth. Therefore they accept scientific theories of evolution.

### Islam
Some Muslims accept the theory of evolution. This is possible because the Qur'an does not talk of time periods during which creation took place, nor does it describe the order in which creation happened.

### Jainism
Jains believe that not only is the universe eternal, but so is everything within it. No one created living things in the universe and no one can destroy them. Jains believe that there are many earths, each going through its own cycles.

### Judaism
There are many different responses to the theory of evolution in Judaism. Some Jews accept that evolution took place and they see G-d as the creator of the process. Others ignore the issue, saying that the creation stories are answering a different question. Jews do not take the creation stories literally.

### Sikhism
Sikhs consider that both science and religion are about discovering the truth. Sikhism accepts the possibility of the truth of both God and the Big Bang. Therefore they accept scientific theories of evolution.

### Zoroastrianism
Evolution can be viewed as a set of stages through which species on the earth came into being. In this way, the theory of evolution can be seen as a natural law in the world. Zoroastrians see natural laws and order as evidence of God's creation.

# Drawing it all together

## Learning about religion

1 Looking at two or more of the religions you have studied, explain what they believe about evolution.

2 Looking at the creation stories which you have studied, what common points can you find in them? Write a paragraph explaining what these stories teach about the relationship between God and humans. In your answer you should also say what is different in the stories.

## Learning from religion

1 Discuss with a partner what you both believe about evolution. Write a short summary to present to the class.

**Hint** Remember to explain the reasons for your opinions.

2 Why might religious believers feel threatened by the theory of evolution?

**Hint** You need to compare the ideas behind religious and non-religious views.

3 In a society it is necessary to look after the weak, the poor and the distressed. How does this fit into Darwin's theory of evolution?

**Hint** Think carefully about your answer and show that you have considered different religious viewpoints.

# 7.3 Are religion and science in conflict?

## Your lesson objectives

**In this lesson you will:**

- discover that science and religion are historically connected
- identify the key areas of disagreement between Christianity and science
- decide whether religion and science are really in conflict.

## Your key words

**Big Bang**

the huge explosion that many people believe led to the formation of the universe

**Creationist**

a person who believes in the factual truth of the creation stories of the Bible and rejects scientific ideas of evolution

When people are asked about what they believe, many people say 'I don't believe in religion, I believe in science!' This type of statement demonstrates that people often think that there is a conflict between religion and science which makes it impossible to follow both. Is this really the case?

## Early scientists

Some of the earliest examples of scientific discoveries come from ancient Greece. Ever since this time, humans have been engaged in the process of trying to find out more about the world around them.

Historically, the Christian Church has been the source of many scientific discoveries, with members of the clergy actively working on scientific experiments and research. As Christians, members of the Church have sought to discover more about the world that God has created. Many believed that a better understanding of the world could lead to a greater understanding of God.

## Conflicts between science and religion

The Church has not always agreed with the outcomes of scientific research. A famous example is that of Galileo (1564–1642).

Galileo was a scientist and astronomer. He used his observations of the stars and planets as evidence to support the idea that the earth revolved around the sun. For many hundreds of years, the Church had taught that the sun, stars and planets revolved around the earth.

The Christian leaders found these scientific views very threatening because they were based on science rather than on the Bible. They saw revelation through reason as challenging the Bible as a Special Revelation. Galileo was arrested and threatened with execution unless he denied that his views were true. Although he did so, he remained under house arrest for the rest of his life.

This well-known example has been used ever since to suggest that religion and science are in conflict. However, the Roman Catholic Church published Galileo's works in 1741 and in 1992 Pope John Paul II said he was sorry for the treatment that Galileo had received.

## Learning about religion

1 Has the Church always been opposed to science?

2 Explain in your own words how Galileo's trial has been used to show that religion and science are in conflict.

Galileo Galilei was put on trial for proposing that the sun was at the centre of the solar system.

## Science and religion today

A key area where Christianity and science appear to clash is creation. Discoveries and theories such as the **Big Bang** or evolution move scientists ever closer to understanding the origins of life. Despite this, the message of Christianity remains unchanged. Although many Christians accept these theories and believe that the questions explored by science and religion are of a different nature, others remain committed to the Bible's account of creation. These Christians are usually called '**Creationists**'. Another area where Christianity and science may appear to clash is over the resurrection of Jesus which cannot be repeated in a scientific test.

So, is it possible to answer the question 'Are science and religion in conflict?' Investigations into the origins of the world are only a tiny part of the work that scientists are currently engaged in. Equally, creation stories are a small part of Christian belief. If these disagreements are left to one side, it is possible to see many areas where Christians approve of and agree with science.

### Your discussion

What conclusion do you reach about whether religion and science are in conflict? Give reasons for your view.

# 7.3 Are religion and science in conflict?

## Bahá'í
Bahá'í teachings stress the unity of science and religion because they believe that there is only one truth. Bahá'u'lláh taught that human intelligence and reasoning were gifts from God.

## Hinduism
Hindus have a range of responses to science. Some see scientific views as perfectly compatible with their religion. Others suggest that scientific truth is subject to human error and can be misleading.

## Islam
Islam does not see a conflict with science as it teaches that science seeks to discover more about the world that Allah has created.

## Judaism
There is no the conflict between Judaism and science. Maimonides was a philosopher who said that when science and religion disagreed this was because one of them was not being understood properly.

## Buddhism
Buddhism does not have particular creation stories and does not see any conflict between religion and science.

## Humanism
Most Humanists do not accept that there is any scientific evidence for the existence of a god. The concept of god or gods therefore has no relevance for their lives.

## Jainism
Jainism is often viewed as one of the most scientific religions in the world and many people find no contradiction between Jain ideas and those put forward by science.

## Sikhism
Sikhs consider that both science and religion are to do with seeking the truth. They aim to be truthful in every area of life. The Sikh *gurus* did not consider scientific research to be a separate part of the search for truth.

## Zoroastrianism
Zoroastrianism does not try to replace scientific thinking, nor does it attempt to provide scientific answers, instead it encourages science. Issues that can be solved with science are seen as small questions best left to science while Zoroastrian teachings focus on much bigger questions.

# Drawing it all together

## Learning about religion

1 Look at two or more of the religions you have studied and write a paragraph on whether they believe that science and religion are in conflict.

2 The Jewish philosopher Maimonides said that when science and religion disagreed it was because one of them was not being understood properly. How do you think the followers of two religions you have studied would respond to this?

## Learning from religion

1 'In schools, pupils should be taught about scientific theories of evolution as well as religious views.' Think carefully about this and make a list showing what you think are the advantages and disadvantages of this system.

**Hint** Try to list a balance of opinions and to give different religious views as well as your own.

2 Do you think that religious creation stories should be taught alongside scientific theories about evolution in school science lessons? Give reasons to support your answer.

**Hint** Consider the advantages and disadvantages of this approach before deciding on your opinion.

3 Should scientists always be allowed to do something simply because they can? Discuss this with a partner and compare your ideas.

**Hint** Remember to consider different religious and non-religious views.

# 7.4 Can a scientist be religious?

## Your lesson objectives

**In this lesson you will:**

- explore the arguments of two scientists with different opinions on the relationship between religion and science

- weigh up the arguments for and against scientists being religious.

## Albert Einstein (1879–1955)

Albert Einstein was Jewish. He was a Humanist and an **agnostic**. He was also a scientific genius. He said that he did not believe in a personal god and that the only way in which he could be called religious would be in his admiration for the structure of the world, as it has been shown through science.

He said that, although religion and science are separate, 'science without religion is lame, religion without science is blind' and so the two cannot truly be in conflict.

## Richard Dawkins (1941– )

Richard Dawkins is a scientist who argues that science and religion cannot both be right. He is an **atheist** and does not agree with religion, either in its teachings or as an organisation. He believes that religion encourages people to be content with not understanding the world.

For Dawkins, religion provides answers that are not really answers at all. He suggests that religions ignore evidence and rely on untested beliefs. As a scientist, Dawkins cannot accept this. He is also concerned that religion causes people to stop investigating the world and encourages them to follow religious teachings instead of trying to discover more about the world. He argues that although some scientists claim to be religious believers, they are rare and surprising.

## Your key words

**agnostic**
someone who believes that some things cannot be fully known

**atheist**
someone who believes there is no God

**commitment**
a sense of being dedicated to something

## Learning about religion

1 Create a table with two columns: 'For' and 'Against'. Try to add as many different arguments as you can on each side to answer the question 'Can a scientist be religious?'

2 If Albert Einstein and Richard Dawkins were able to meet, what do you think they might say to one another about science and religion?

**Albert Einstein was a scientific genius.**

## Religious scientists and scientific believers?

As Dawkins notes, many scientists today claim to be religious. Scientists such as Sir John Polkinghorne and Arthur Peacocke have defended the relationship between science and religious belief. This would indicate that although sometimes religion and science are in conflict, many people do combine their belief in God with their **commitment** to science. As Einstein argued, belief can actually encourage scientific exploration.

On the other hand, many scientists are not religious. They may agree with Dawkins that religion cannot offer the answers they seek and so they rely on science to help them understand the world using experiments and research.

It has been suggested that neither religion nor science claims to give a full account of the world. If this is the case, then it may be sensible for people to combine some elements of both approaches to create their own world views.

# 7.4 Can a scientist be religious?

### Bahá'í
Bahá'ís say that it is not possible for something to be scientifically false and religiously true. Therefore there is no problem with a scientist being religious.

### Buddhism

Most Buddhists do not see any problem with being both a scientist and following the *Dhamma/Dharma*. As long as the study of science does not interfere with an individual's Buddhist practices, it is acceptable.

### Hinduism
Hindus offer different views about whether science and religion are compatible. Some consider the belief that life emerges from matter is inconsistent with Hindu ideas of an eternal self. Others consider science and Hinduism to be perfectly compatible.

### Humanism
Many scientists are Humanists. This may be because they have an atheist or agnostic point of view.

### Jainism
The nature of Jainism is to be inquisitive and search for truth. Following truth in everyday life is given the highest importance, therefore there is no reason for a Jain not to be a scientist.

### Islam

Islam was a major factor in the development of science from its beginning. Islamic scholars were famed for their scientific knowledge and discoveries and Muslim scientists and doctors have continued to be at the forefront of developments.

### Sikhism

Sikhism teaches that there are limitless worlds and that God can be approached in many different ways. There are other worlds and there may be intelligent and indeed religious life on other planets. Therefore, Sikhs welcome the work of scientists and scientific discovery.

### Judaism
Judaism sees very few problems in relation to modern scientific discoveries, particularly in to the area of medical science. There are many Jewish scientists who practise their faith.

### Zoroastrianism

Many Zoroastrians are scientists and do not find any conflict between their scientific knowledge and their religion. For example, when the positive and negative aspects of electricity were discovered this was seen to be in line with religious beliefs about the opposites of good and evil.

# Drawing it all together

## Learning about religion

1 Looking at two or more of the religions you have studied, what do you think their attitudes would be towards someone being a scientist? Give explanations for your answer.

2 Choose one area to focus on, such as health, and think of any circumstances when we should not make use of science even though it is available to us. Look at the views of the religions you have studied and write a paragraph in response to this question.

## Learning from religion

1 Do you think there are ways in which science can help people to understand religion? Give examples to illustrate your opinion.

**Hint** Think about the views held by religions you have studied and how science might influence these.

2 'There are some questions that science cannot answer, and some that science cannot address.' Explain what you think this statement means and whether it is true.

**Hint** Think carefully about the differences between these two suggestions. It may be that you think one is true and the other not.

3 Working with a partner create a presentation with the title: 'Can a scientist be religious?'

**Hint** Remember to consider different religious and non-religious views and to explain them.

# 7.5 Creating life: IVF, cloning and genetic engineering

## Your lesson objectives

**In this lesson you will:**

- connect Christian beliefs about God with the attitudes of Christians towards IVF, cloning and genetic engineering.

## Your key words

**cloning**

a process that involves creating replicas of living beings or parts of them

**embryo**

a fertilised egg

**in-vitro fertilisation (IVF)**

a process that involves creating an embryo outside the womb

## God as the Creator

The Bible teaches that God created the world and everything in it. Many Christians would connect the human urge to create things with the belief that humans have been made in the 'image of God'. Humans are not able to create things out of nothing as God does, but Christians believe that they can still have a role in the ongoing creation of the world.

'It is better to create than to learn! Creating is the essence of life.'
(Julius Caesar)
Do you agree with this statement?

## Creating life

The Bible teaches that God not only first created life on earth, but also plays a part in the creation of all human beings: 'For you created my inmost being; you knit me together in my mother's womb' (Psalm 139:13).

When scientists are involved in procedures such as **in-vitro fertilisation (IVF)**, **cloning** or genetic engineering, they are seeking to help in this process of creating life.

The first book of the Bible, Genesis, tells Christians that God expects them to have children. Having children is seen as an important part of marriage and most Christians would seek to create a family of their own. However, many couples find themselves unable to have children naturally. IVF is a process that helps people to have a baby by fertilising the egg in a laboratory before placing it back into the mother's womb so that she becomes pregnant.

Not all Christians agree on the topic of IVF. Some Christians, including many Protestants, would argue that by using IVF scientists are simply helping a couple to fulfil God's wish for them to have children. Other Christians, including the Roman Catholic Church, would disagree with this approach. They believe that pregnancy should occur naturally. IVF interferes in what should be a natural occurrence when a woman and a man have a sexual relationship. They also do not approve of the creation of 'spare' **embryos** which are later destroyed.

## Learning about religion

Copy out the two quotes from the Bible. Now explain in your own words what each one tells Christians about God's role in creation.

## Your discussion

Do you think that it is possible to create a true replica of a human being? Consider identical twins. Are they ever really identical? What makes humans unique?

## Cloning and genetic engineering

Cloning and genetic research can be used to develop treatments for diseases, helping to save and improve human lives. However, sometimes these types of research involve creating embryos that are then destroyed. The Bible teaches that all humans are unique: 'And even the very hairs of your head are all numbered' (Matthew 10:30).

As some Christians believe that God is involved in the creation of all life and that life should be seen as a gift from him, they would be concerned about these procedures and would avoid them whenever possible.

# 7.5 Creating life: IVF, cloning and genetic engineering

### Bahá'í
The Bahá'í Faith does not have any objections to the use of scientific advances such as infertility treatment provided that it is carried out with proper respect for the new life being created.

### Hinduism
Traditionally, a childless couple might adopt an infant from a close family member. These days, many couples see IVF as acceptable. Fewer Hindus accept the use of donor sperm in IVF, as there is then no link between a father and his child.

### Islam
Muslims believe that science has a role to play in life, helping people to understand the world Allah has created. Treatments like IVF can be a part of this process but ultimately it is Allah's will that decides what happens in life.

### Judaism
Judaism supports most forms of treatment that medical advances allow. *Rabbis* have permitted IVF as long as the egg and sperm are those of the couple. However, Judaism does not permit the use of donor eggs or sperm, because this could lead to confusion over who is the mother or father of the child.

### Buddhism
At the time of the Buddha, nothing was known about advances in medical science such as IVF. Buddhists now have to consider whether they might cause harm to others or waste potential human lives.

### Humanism
Humanists respect life but, as they are not religious, they do not accept the idea of the sanctity of life or worry that scientists are 'playing God'.

### Jainism
All living beings are considered important to Jains but human life is given the highest importance. Jains accept that science can provide new knowledge and can advance human knowledge for the good of humanity but Jains believe this should not be abused.

### Sikhism
Sikhism welcomes medical advances that help to protect life. Sikh couples who cannot have a child naturally can consider IVF as long as it is the husband's sperm that is used to fertilise the egg. Sikhs would not agree to use donor eggs or sperm as this would break the bond between a husband and wife.

### Zoroastrianism
All suffering, including infertility, is believed to come from evil. Treatments that help infertile couples have children are seen as a way of responding to this.

# Drawing it all together

## Learning about religion

1  Looking at two or more of the religions you have studied, explain what they believe about the use of fertility treatment.

2  Do you think that religions might have different attitudes towards cloning than they do to the use of infertility treatment? Give reasons for your answer.

## Learning from religion

1  If plants can be genetically modified to produce more food is this a good idea? Explain your own opinion and what religious believers might think.

**Hint** Remember to consider the possible good and bad effects of genetically modified crops.

2  Is it helpful to consider problems like infertility as being the result of a lack of balance in creation?

**Hint** How might this idea affect religious and non-religious views on the use of these treatments?

3  'Medicine should not interfere with God's will.' Discuss this with a partner. Make a list of points for and against the statement.

**Hint** You could organise a debate in class and take a vote on this.

# 7.6 Should we use animals for experiments?

## Your lesson objectives

**In this lesson you will:**

- recognise Christian arguments for the difference between humans and animals

- connect Christian beliefs with their attitude towards animal experimentation.

## Your key words

**flourish**

to develop in a positive, healthy way

**soul**

the spiritual part of a human regarded as immortal

**stewardship**

looking after something for someone else

## The place of animals

It is impossible to know exactly how many animals there are in the world. Scientists have identified 1.5 million different species, but many millions more have yet to be classified and there are probably more still to be found. In contrast, there is only one human species on earth. Most Christians would argue that humans have a special place in the world.

The idea that humans are different from all other animals is found in the Bible. Humans were created 'in the image of God' (Genesis 1:27). From the Bible Christians learn about their responsibility for planet earth and their place in the 'Community of Creation'.

## Protecting animals

Although not believing that animals have **souls**, Christians believe that they are still part of God's creation. The Book of Genesis describes how God created all living creatures, blessed them and said to them: 'Be fruitful and increase in number and fill the water in the seas, and let the birds increase in the earth' (Genesis 1:22).

In accordance with this, Christians believe that, like humans, animals should be able to **flourish** on the earth. Humans have a role to ensure that this is possible. This protective role is called **stewardship**.

As stewards of the world, humans have a duty to take care of the world and everything in it. In the biblical story of Noah and the flood, Noah is asked to take a male and a female of every animal on earth with him into the Ark, protecting them just as he did his own family. This shows how humans have a role to play in the protection of animals.

## Protection and experimentation

Although Christians believe that they have a responsibility to take care of animals, they also have a role to protect each other.

Today, science is able to create medicines and treatments to protect people from disease and death. As a part of the testing of these treatments, animals are often experimented on. Many scientists argue that these tests are essential and that without them people would die. Christians are against the mistreatment of animals, but if animal testing saves lives, many Christians would accept that they have been given the right to use animals in this way.

Just like stewards at a large concert or football game, the role of Christians is to protect and help others.

# 7.6 Should we use animals for experiments?

## Bahá'í
The Bahá'í Faith teaches that animals should be treated with kindness. Bahá'u'lláh said that kindness to animals is one of the qualities which must be acquired by anyone searching for God. Animal experiments should be minimal and avoid unnecessary suffering.

## Hinduism
Hindus follow the principle of *ahimsa* (non-violence). They believe that animals have an *atman* (soul), since they too feel pleasure and pain and emotions like fear and affection. For these reasons, most Hindus disapprove of experiments on animals.

## Islam
The Qur'an describes how humans were put on earth with a duty of stewardship. If research on animals is essential to create medicines that save or improve lives, then many Muslims would accept this, although the animals used in testing these medicines must not suffer unnecessarily.

## Judaism
Jews do not see animals as having the same rights as humans. They believe that humans have been given power over animals but they are still required to respect them. Animals can be used to benefit humanity but should not be abused or caused pain or suffering.

## Buddhism
The principle of *ahimsa* means that Buddhists will try to avoid harming any living being by practising 'right action'. Animal experiments, particularly those with no medical basis, would be a harmful action.

## Humanism
Humanists try to make decisions by using reason and compassion. They do not tolerate cruelty and prefer not to cause unnecessary suffering to animals. Humanists differ in their views about the use of animals in experiments.

## Jainism
Jainism teaches that all living things have *jivas* or souls and they value all living things including animals. Jains believe there is no reason why animals need to be used for experiments.

## Sikhism
To decide on difficult issues such as animal experimentation, Sikhs must look to their consciences in applying Sikh teaching. Sikhism teaches that people should not cause suffering to other beings so Sikhs must weigh up the arguments in order to act in a way that they feel is right.

## Zoroastrianism
The Zoroastrian holy book, the Avesta, condemns the mistreatment of animals. The good treatment of animals is viewed as a 'good deed' by Zoroastrians. Using animals in experiments is allowed but to harm them would be a sin.

# Drawing it all together

## Learning about religion

**1** Looking at two of the religions you have studied, describe and explain their attitudes towards animal experiments.

**2** Write a paragraph about the idea of stewardship and include your own opinions as well as religious ones.

## Learning from religion

**1** Look at the relationships humans have with other animals. Make two lists headed 'Use' and 'Abuse'.

**Hint** Use the information you have learnt to show how your views compare to the religious teachings you have studied.

**2** Under what circumstances do you think it is right to take an animal's life? Discuss this with a partner and share your views as a class.

**Hint** In your answer you should consider different religious and non-religious views as well as giving your own view.

**3** Imagine that everyone followed the teaching of *ahimsa* (non-violence). Working with a partner try to think of as many things as you can which might change in the world.

**Hint** You need to look at all aspects of life both in the UK and elsewhere.

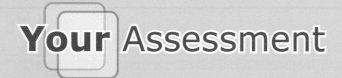

# Your Assessment

Compare the views of different religions about how religion and science can be of benefit to each other.

**Hint** You need to look first at the different ways in which religion and science can help each other.

# 8 Can we all get on?

## The bigger picture

There are around seven billion people living on the earth. Every single one of them is different. Even identical twins have minor differences, some of them too small for anyone to notice. For most people, the differences do not affect the way they live. However, some people focus on the differences, thinking that a certain type of person is better than another for no other reason than the way they look. This is called prejudice – pre-judging a person or group without getting to know them. This may be based on the way a person looks rather than on who they are and how they behave. Even minor differences in the way people look and how they live can become targets for people who are prejudiced. Whatever the difference, it is unlikely to be the victim's fault.

Prejudice can cause harm and distress to its victims, ranging from being made to feel uncomfortable to loss of life.

This chapter considers various prejudices that people may hold, investigates why some people are prejudiced and looks at the harm that prejudice can cause.

1 Make a list of six things that make people different. Do these differences matter? Say why.

2 Think about what life would be like if everybody was the same. Would life be better? Why?

**Your discussion**

'Everybody is equal.'
Do you think this
is always true?

# 8 Introduction Can we all get on?

## Your lesson objectives

**In this lesson you will:**

- understand the difference between prejudice and discrimination
- analyse Christian teachings about prejudice and discrimination.

## Your key words

**discrimination**

treating someone unfairly because they belong to a particular group or class

**evidence**

facts that can be used as proof

**gender**

the characteristics that are different in male and female

**opinion**

someone's personal view on a subject

**prejudice**

an opinion formed without knowledge or reason

**stereotyping**

taking a generalised, oversimplified view of a group of people, which is usually negative

## What are prejudice and discrimination?

At some time in their life, many people are the victims of **prejudice** – other people form opinions of them, based for example on how they look, how they dress, how they talk or where they live. Prejudice is pre-judging a person or group without getting to know them. In other words, some people make judgements about individuals or groups without any **evidence** to base these judgements on.

**Stereotyping** has a part to play in prejudice. For example, the stereotype of an elderly person may be that they are rather slow, hard of hearing and generally old-fashioned. While some may fall into this stereotype, many do not. Treating people as if they fit a stereotype would probably cause offence and upset them, because it is prejudiced and wrong.

Sometimes, people allow their prejudices to affect what they do. They may treat someone in a certain way, based on their **opinion** of the sort of person they believe them to be and not the sort of person they really are. This is called **discrimination** – actions based on prejudiced thoughts. There are many examples of this, including racism (discrimination based on race), sexism (discrimination based on **gender**) and ageism (discrimination based on age – young or old). None of these categories can be changed by the person involved and prejudiced thoughts can turn into actions that are unfair and wrong.

## What do Christians think about prejudice and discrimination?

Christian teachings are firmly against prejudice. Jesus taught this in the Parable of the Good Samaritan (Luke 10:25–37) and also said '… in the same way as you judge others, you will be judged and with the measure you use, it will be measured to you' (Matthew 7:2b).

St Paul wrote a letter to the Church in Galatia in around 50 CE. In it he wrote: 'There is neither Jew nor Greek, slave nor free, male nor female, for you are all one in Christ Jesus' (Galatians 3:28).

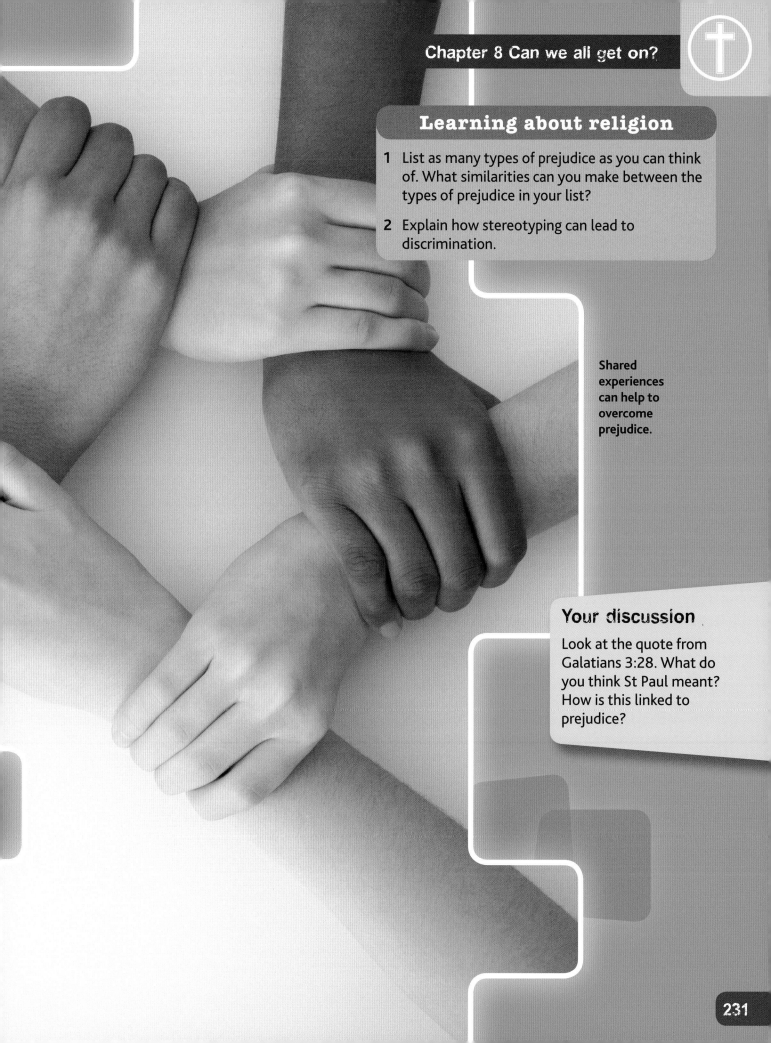

## Learning about religion

1 List as many types of prejudice as you can think of. What similarities can you make between the types of prejudice in your list?

2 Explain how stereotyping can lead to discrimination.

Shared experiences can help to overcome prejudice.

## Your discussion

Look at the quote from Galatians 3:28. What do you think St Paul meant? How is this linked to prejudice?

# 8 Introduction Can we all get on?

## Bahá'í
A central belief in the Bahá'í Faith is in the unity of humankind. People are all the children of God with the divine spark within each person. Whatever race, religion or gender, all people are one.

## Buddhism
The whole of Buddhist teaching and practice is designed to overcome attachment to the world and to ideas which have no foundation, such as prejudice. A person working towards enlightenment must not be prejudiced.

## Hinduism
Hinduism has long taught that there is spiritual equality but has tried to allow for diversity through the system of four *varnas* (social classes). Originally this system seems to have allowed social mobility but later became the caste system, with inherited positions in society and unfair treatment of some groups. Today, caste practice is gradually being removed.

## Humanism
Humanists believe that, as humans have evolved as a species, they share the same ancestors, so everyone is distantly related to each other. People should learn to live together in harmony, regardless of race, colour, gender, religion etc.

## Islam
Muslims believe that Allah created all life including humans. As a result, everyone should be treated well and differences between people should not lead to discrimination.

## Jainism
The supreme principle of Jain living is *ahimsa* (wherever possible, not causing any harm). As prejudice causes harm that is intentional, it is considered to be wrong.

## Judaism
Jews believe that G-d created all living creatures. In the Torah, the Jews are told to treat strangers living among them with respect – 'You shall love him as yourself' (Leviticus 19:34).

## Sikhism
Everybody is created by God, even though there are differences between individuals. These differences should not be used as an excuse for prejudice.

## Zoroastrianism
Zoroastrians believe that humans should choose to help God to remove evil from the earth. They believe that all humans are equal, regardless of race, gender, age etc., and that prejudice is helping evil and not good.

# Drawing it all together

## Learning about religion

1 Explain what the religions you have studied teach about prejudice.

2 What is the difference between prejudice and discrimination?

## Learning from religion

1 Do you think that religious believers should be prejudiced in favour of their own religion? Explain why.

**Hint** Think about whether prejudice is always wrong.

2 Do you agree that prejudice only becomes a problem when it leads to discrimination? Give your reasons.

**Hint** Think about whether there is a difference between thought and action.

3 Should everybody be treated equally? Explain your answer.

**Hint** Are poor people equal to rich people?

# 8.1 The way forward

## Your lesson objectives

In this lesson you will:

- consider how religions get on with each other
- understand the effects of religious prejudice.

## Your key words

**denomination**

a branch of a religion

**faith**

belief in somebody or something especially without logical proof

**pacifism**

using peaceful methods to achieve an aim

**persecuted**

someone being punished because of, for example, their beliefs

## How do religions get on with each other?

History shows that, over the years, some religions have struggled to get on with some others.

- Many early Christians were **persecuted** by Jews who wanted to prevent Christianity from spreading. One of the main persecutors was Saul who, after seeing a vision of Jesus, became a Christian and changed his name to Paul. He became one of the most important early Christian leaders.

- The Crusades were fought between Christians and Muslims in the 11th to 13th centuries.

- Sikhism had to change its views on **pacifism** when faced with persecution from some Muslim rulers.

Nowadays, there still seem to be conflicts between religions and these are often more complicated than they appear. In some cases, people who say they are fighting for their **faith** are actually interpreting parts of their faith in a way that most would disagree with.

Unfortunately, religious prejudice has had a negative effect on millions of people when wars fought between different faiths have caused casualties, and religious terrorism has caused people to live in fear.

Often, groups or **denominations** within a single religion show prejudice towards each other. From 1969 to 1998, around 3250 people died in conflicts between Roman Catholic and Protestant groups in Northern Ireland. Each side in the dispute had political aims as well as religious ones.

## What are Christian attitudes to other religions?

Many Christians consider that other religions display the way God reveals himself through various cultures, but that the central message of Jesus and his special relationship with God sets Christians apart from other believers. This can be seen as meaning that Jesus provides access to God for those who choose to be Christians and show unconditional love for God and other people, but that other religions provide the same access for their followers if they show the same unconditional love.

Connect: different faiths shared values is an interfaith action and resource guide for young people.

## Learning about religion

1 Give examples of religions not getting on with each other.

2 Why do people of the same religion and people of different religions criticise each other?

3 How might religious prejudice affect a religious believer? Would it affect a non-believer in the same way? Explain your answer.

# Connect

## different faiths shared values

## Your discussion

'Having respect for the differences between them helps religions to get on with each other better.'

Do you think this is always true?

## Working together

There are several organisations that try to bring different faiths together. In the UK, one of the largest of these is the Inter Faith Network:

The Inter Faith Network for the UK was founded in 1987 to promote good relations between people of different faiths in this country. …

The Network works with its member bodies to help make the UK a place marked by mutual understanding and respect between religions where all can practise their faith with integrity.

# 8.1 The way forward

### Bahá'í
Bahá'ís believe that the different faiths that exist in the world are all approaches to the same God. There should therefore be no difficulties between Bahá'ís and members of other faiths.

### Buddhism
Buddhists tend to focus on the similarities between Buddhism and other religions rather than on the differences between them. They believe that working together is important.

### Hinduism
Hindus believe that all religions relate to the same God. Hindus accept members of other religious traditions, provided they do not use religion in ways that are selfish or exclude other sections of society.

### Humanism
Most Humanists believe that people should respect the views of others and treat them with consideration. There are many Humanists, though, who would like the influence religion has on society to be reduced.

### Islam
There is disagreement about other religions between Muslims. Some believe Islam is the only true faith whereas others believe that as there is one God anybody who worships him will achieve Paradise. Most Muslims, regardless of what they believe, will try to get on with other believers.

### Jainism
Jains do not see other religions as a threat to their existence. Indeed, they are keen to work with other religions, especially Hinduism and Buddhism. This is because they share some beliefs and traditions with these two religions.

### Judaism
Jews make it clear that even though there are very important differences between Judaism and other religions, contact between people of all religions is important, especially to discuss vital issues such as war and peace.

### Sikhism
Sikhs believe that all religions lead to God so it does not really matter which religion a person follows. If they follow it properly, they will achieve salvation.

### Zoroastrianism
Zoroastrianism has a respectful approach to other religions and ways of life and although small in number, their message of 'Good thoughts, good words and good deeds' remains strong.

# Drawing it all together

## Learning about religion

1 Write a short paragraph to show what the religions you have learnt about teach about the way they should treat other religions.

2 Explain how the different religions found in UK society might affect everyone's life.

## Learning from religion

1 Some people would like there to be just one religion in the world. Explain some of the reasons they may give for thinking this.

**Hint** Think about problems that exist between religions

2 Do you think the influence religion has on the world should be reduced? Say why.

**Hint** Think of ways religion influences the world both for good and for bad.

3 If there was only enough money to build one place of worship in a town where there were members of three religions, what do you think would be the result?

**Hint** What would be the advantages and disadvantages of shared places of worship?

# 8.2 Are women and men equal?

## Your lesson objectives

**In this lesson you will:**

- investigate issues of equality between women and men

- evaluate the idea that men and women have different roles.

It is usually assumed that men and women are equal. The first creation story in Genesis 1:27–8 says:

> So God created man in his own image, in the image of God he created him; male and female he created them.

> God blessed them and said to them, 'Be fruitful and increase in number; fill the earth and subdue it. Rule over the fish of the sea and the birds of the air and over every living creature that moves on the ground.'

This suggests that men and women have equal roles in being in charge of the earth. However, the second creation story, found in Genesis 2, gives a different view of the role of women:

> But for Adam no suitable helper was found. So the LORD God caused the man to fall into a deep sleep; and while he was sleeping, he took one of the man's ribs and closed up the place with flesh. Then the Lord God made a woman from the rib he had taken out of the man, and he brought her to the man.

> (Genesis 2:20b–2)

This version of the story seems to be saying that Eve – the first woman – was created as a helper for Adam. Later, when they were thrown out of the Garden of Eden, God said to Eve that as part of her punishment: 'Your desire will be for your husband, and he will rule over you' (Genesis 3:16b).

However, elsewhere in both the Old and New Testaments there are references to men and women being joined as one flesh in marriage or in Jesus. This implies that men and women are equal and not that men are in some way more important than women. It has also been suggested that Jesus' resurrection lifted the punishment placed on Adam and Eve.

No matter whether men and women are equal, few would deny that men and women should have equal **rights**. The Universal Declaration of Human Rights makes this clear and there are very few countries in the world which have not signed and adopted the Declaration.

## Your key words

**right**
the moral or legal claim to have or do something

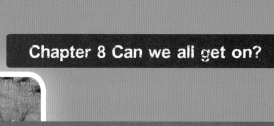

## Learning about religion

1 Explain how the Genesis creation stories can be interpreted as teaching that women are not equal to men.

2 Do you agree with this way of thinking? Why?

3 Do you think it is right that men and women should have different roles? Why?

## Should men and women have different roles?

In the past, in most societies women have had different roles from men. Traditionally, men have gone out to work and women have stayed at home raising children. In some societies, this still happens. However, in many countries including the UK, where Christianity has had the most influence on the culture, such attitudes are changing. The number of women working for a living, whether or not their husband or partner also works, is increasing.

*The Garden of Eden* by Hieronymus Bosch, c.1500. What caused God to punish Adam and Eve?

## Your discussion

'Equality and equal rights do not mean that men and women are the same.'

Is this true? Give reasons for your answer.

# 8.2 Are women and men equal?

## Bahá'í
Bahá'ís believe in full equality between women and men. Male and female characteristics, whilst different, are equally valuable, so women and men should share equal rights and freedoms.

## Hinduism
The Laws of Manu teach that wives should serve their husbands, and husbands must protect and cherish their wives. Some have interpreted the first part of this as encouraging mistreatment of women. Today, both Hindu men and women are breaking away from such traditional roles.

## Islam
According to the Qur'an, women and men are considered equal in the sight of Allah. Both women and men will be accepted into Paradise if they live a life pleasing to Allah. They do have different roles though, the woman in the home caring for her family and the man providing for his wife and family.

## Judaism
Jews believe that women and men are created equal but they have different roles. The traditional role of a woman is to be a wife and mother while the man is supposed to pray and study. Both are important but some believe that the role of the woman is more important.

## Buddhism
Most Buddhists believe that women and men have the same chance of spiritual advancement, earned on their own merit. Both can become enlightened.

## Humanism
The belief that all people should be treated as individuals is central for Humanists. This means that women and men have a right to be treated equally without any stereotyping or discrimination.

## Jainism
While most Jains believe in equality between women and men, some do not. Although many accept that both women and men can achieve *moksha* (liberation), Digambara Jains believe that only men can do this. Equality is seen in relation to *moksha* rather than everyday life.

## Sikhism
Guru Nanak Dev Ji made it very clear that women and men should be treated equally because they are equal in the eyes of God. Despite this, many Sikh women take the role of homemaker, whilst their husbands provide for them and their family.

## Zoroastrianism
Zoroastrians believe that women and men were created together when they both emerged from a plant and are equal in every respect. They both share the gift of consciousness in being able to think and reason.

# Drawing it all together

## Learning about religion

1 What do the religions you have learnt about teach about whether women and men are equal?

2 Explain why some religious people do not see men and women as equal.

## Learning from religion

1 Does having different roles in religion for women and men mean they are not equal? Explain your thoughts on this.

**Hint** Think of how important these different roles are.

2 'You cannot be a religious person and not treat men and women equally.' Do you agree? Explain why/why not.

**Hint** Try to think about different opinions before deciding which you agree with.

3 Why do you think most religions refer to God as male? Give as many reasons as you can.

**Hint** Think about the alternative ways of referring to God and what religious people believe God has done.

# 8.3 What is the role of men and women in worship?

## Your lesson objectives

**In this lesson you will:**

- understand that traditionally men and women have different roles in worship

- recognise and analyse changing attitudes in some Christian denominations.

## Your key words

**Bible**

a word used for the sacred writings of the Jews (Tenakh) and Christians (Old and New Testaments)

**Eucharist**

a service celebrating the sacrifice of the death and resurrection of Jesus Christ, using bread and wine. This is sometimes called Holy Communion (Protestant), Liturgy (Orthodox) or Mass (Roman Catholic)

**priest**

a person with the authority to perform religious ceremonies

**sacrament**

a religious ceremony which is the outward visible sign of an inward spiritual grace

**worship**

to show love, respect or devotion to someone or something

Traditionally in Christianity, men and women have been allowed to worship together, but the leader of worship – the **priest** – was always male. One of the reasons given for this was that, because Jesus and his 12 disciples were all men, it was assumed that God required faith leaders to be male. They were following on from Jesus, especially in celebrating the **sacrament** of the **Eucharist**.

Women have been allowed to play a minor role in **worship** by doing such things as reading from the **Bible**, playing the organ or singing in the choir. However, many Free Churches have had women ministers for over 200 years and attitudes towards women as religious leaders are changing across the world.

The Roman Catholic Church insist that priests must be male and remain unmarried, because they are supposed to be married to the Church. If they were married, their loyalties would be divided between their wife and the Church, and both could suffer. It seems unlikely that the Roman Catholic Church will ordain women as priests or allow priests to be married in the near future.

Other Catholic Churches such as the Orthodox Church do have married male priests.

In 1992, the Church of England, following pressure from interested individuals and groups, decided to allow women to become priests. Their role is the same as any male priest, including celebrating the Eucharist. There has been opposition to this decision and some members of the Church of England have decided to become Roman Catholics as a result.

By 2006, more women than men were ordained as Church of England priests, although as yet no woman has become a bishop in the UK.

Canon Jane Hedges at a service of evening prayer at Westminster Abbey, 2010. Since 1992 the Church of England has ordained women as priests.

## Learning about religion

1   Explain why, traditionally, Christian priests have always been male.

2   Do you agree that Roman Catholic priests should not be allowed to marry? Give your reasons.

3   Do you agree with the decision the Church of England made in 1992? Explain why.

4   Is there a role for sexism in religion?

## Your discussion

'As all of Jesus' disciples were men, only men should lead Christian worship.'

Do you think this is a valid argument?

# 8.3 What is the role of men and women in worship?

### Bahá'í

All Bahá'ís, whether male or female, are required to recite one of three prayers each day. There are no priests. Bahá'ís meet every 19 days for community worship and fellowship. Active service in the community, which can be done by men or women, is an important part of worship.

### Hinduism

Hindus believe that men and women have equal access to God. Men and women often worship together, although there is respectful separation of the sexes in some temples.

### Islam

In Islam, men and women often worship in separate rooms. The prayers said in the men's prayer hall are broadcast in the women's prayer hall so they can pray as men do. Most *imams* are male and women are not allowed to preach the Friday sermon.

### Judaism

In Orthodox Judaism, men and women are separated during prayer. It is thought by many that women should not lead worship or read from the Torah. Progressive Jews believe G-d has given men and women equal status in worship so they can worship together and women can become *rabbi*s.

### Buddhism

Buddhist men and women show devotion and meditate together in the same room either at home or in a *vihara* (monastery) or temple. Meditation can be led by either a man or a woman without any distinction.

### Humanism

As Humanists believe in the equality and unity of humankind, and not in a god, there is no need for worship.

### Jainism

Svetambara Jains allow the same forms of worship for both men and women. Digambara Jains do not ordain women and women do not take part in temple worship. Women are allowed inside the temples but usually do not touch the images.

### Sikhism

Although Sikh men and women have similar roles in worship and are allowed to worship together, they sit apart while doing so. Women are allowed to lead worship and read the Guru Granth Sahib Ji aloud in the *gurdwara*.

### Zoroastrianism

Zoroaster taught that men and women should pray five times a day. Women are not allowed to become priests although they are allowed to perform various ceremonies and rituals.

# Drawing it all together

## Learning about religion

**1** What do the religions you have learnt about believe about the roles of men and women in worship?

**2** Do you think women should be allowed to lead worship? Explain why/why not.

## Learning from religion

**1** 'Men and women should worship separately so the men are not distracted by the women.' What do you think about this statement? Explain your answer.

**Hint** Try to think about all aspects of the statement before coming to a decision.

**2** Make a list of reasons why people believe men and women should and should not worship together.

**Hint** Try to think of reasons for two different points of view.

**3** 'Giving different roles in worship to men and women is prejudice.' Do you agree?

**Hint** Think carefully about the views of different religions before answering.

**Your Assessment**

What do the religions you have learned about say about predudice?

**Hint** Think carefully about the views of different religions before answering.

# Glossary

**abortion** the deliberate ending of a pregnancy by removal and destruction of the foetus *(page 152)*

**adultery** a sexual relationship between a married person and someone to whom they are not married *(page 156)*

**agnostic** someone who believes that some things cannot be fully known *(pages 72, 216)*

**ancestor** an earlier member of a species that present-day examples are descended from *(page 208)*

**apartheid** separation into different racial groups *(page 148)*

**atheist** someone who believes there is no god *(pages 72, 130, 216)*

**atonement** Jesus' death and resurrection removed the sins of humanity and mended the relationship between people and God *(page 84)*

**atmosphere** a layer of gases surrounding the earth *(page 170)*

**authority** the power or right to be a leader of others *(pages 4, 194)*

**baptism** a ceremony which cleanses a person of Original Sin and welcomes them into the Church *(pages 42, 118)*

**belief** accepting that something is true or real *(pages 16, 26, 69, 130, 152, 174, 204)*

**Bible** a word used for the sacred writing of the Jews (Tenakh) and Christians (Old and New Testaments) *(pages 4, 26, 72, 118, 136, 174, 204, 242)*

**Big Bang** the huge explosion that many people believe led to the formation of the universe *(page 212)*

**celebration** a joyful occasion where an event is marked or remembered *(page 47)*

**charisma** a natural ability to inspire others *(page 8)*

**civilian** someone who is not a member of the armed forces *(page 190)*

**cloning** a process that involves creating replicas of living beings or parts of them *(page 220)*

**commitment** a sense of being dedicated to something *(pages 26, 216)*

**community** a group of people who share something in common *(pages 12, 26, 114, 140, 182, 208)*

**compassion** sympathy and care for something or someone *(page 126)*

**compassionate** showing sympathy and care for others *(page 164)*

**complex** made up of many parts; complicated *(page 72)*

**conceived** the moment when an egg is fertilised by a sperm producing a new life *(page 160)*

**conscience** a knowledge of right and wrong which helps people make decisions *(pages 92, 136, 194, 204)*

**conscientious objector** a person who refuses to fight in a war because of their beliefs *(page 194)*

**contraception** the deliberate use of methods to prevent pregnancy *(page 152)*

**covet** want to possess something *(page 140)*

**Creationist** a person who believes in the factual truth of the creation stories of the Bible and rejects scientific ideas of evolution *(page 212)*

**creed** a statement of belief *(page 34)*

**crucified** fastened to a cross and left to die – a form of execution used by the Romans *(pages 16, 34, 88)*

**denomination** a branch of a religion *(pages 4, 26, 156, 194, 234)*

**developed world** countries with high levels of national income, education, life expectancy and similar benefits *(page 170)*

**developing world** countries with lower levels than developed countries of benefits such as national income, education and life expectancy *(page 170)*

**devotion** loving or being dedicated to something or someone *(page 26)*

**discrimination** treating someone unfairly because they belong to a particular group or class *(pages 148, 230)*

**divine** coming from God *(page 152)*

**DNA** (deoxyribonucleic acid) the material in cells that contains all the 'instructions' for their development *(page 92)*

**doctrine** teaching *(page 80)*

**dominion** being in charge of, or having power over, something *(page 174)*

**embryo** a fertilised egg *(page 220)*

**emotive** causing an emotional response *(page 38)*

**environment** surroundings *(pages 130, 174)*

**eternal life** life after death *(page 140)*

**Eucharist** a service celebrating the sacrifice of the death and resurrection of Jesus Christ, using bread and wine. This is sometimes called Holy Communion (Protestant), Liturgy (Orthodox) or Mass (Roman Catholic) *(pages 4, 42, 242)*

**euthanasia** literally, an 'easy' or 'gentle' death: ending a life painlessly to relieve suffering *(page 152)*

**evidence** facts that can be used as proof *(pages 26, 69, 170, 200, 230)*

**exploit** to use another person or thing for your own advantage *(pages 130, 140)*

**fact** something that can be proved to be true *(pages 30, 130, 144, 200)*

**faith** belief in somebody or something especially without logical proof *(pages 20, 27, 69, 122, 148, 234)*

**flourish** to develop in a positive, healthy way *(page 224)*

**foetus** a young animal in the egg or womb *(page 160)*

**forgiveness** no longer feeling anger or resentment towards someone who has caused you suffering *(pages 62, 122)*

**fossil record** examples of organisms that lived and died some time ago, preserved in rocks *(page 208)*

**free will** the power to act and make choices for yourself *(pages 110, 136)*

**gender** the characteristics that are different in male and female *(page 230)*

**global warming** an increase in the temperature of the earth *(page 171)*

**gospels** the first four books in the New Testament *(page 20)*

**greenhouse effect** the trapping of the sun's heat in the earth's atmosphere, which many scientists believe is causing global warming *(page 171)*

**greenhouse gases** gases that contribute to the greenhouse effect, for example methane and carbon dioxide *(page 182)*

**Heaven** a place of paradise and reward in the presence of God *(pages 16, 80, 152)*

**Hell** eternal life without God *(page 84)*

**Holy Spirit** one person of the Trinity, the other two being the Father and Son *(pages 34, 80)*

**homophobia** prejudice against homosexuals and/or homosexuality *(page 148)*

**immanent** the belief that God is within every human and so involved in the world *(page 80)*

**infallible** not capable of being wrong *(page 4)*

**injustice** unfairness, when people are not treated correctly *(pages 104, 126, 140)*

**in-vitro fertilisation (IVF)** a process that involves creating an embryo outside the womb *(page 220)*

**just cause** a reason that is morally right *(page 190)*

**Just War theory** a set of conditions first put forward by St Thomas Aquinas to decide whether it is right to fight a war *(page 190)*

**landfill site** a place where large quantities of rubbish are buried *(page 182)*

**Levite** in Judaism, a person who is a member of the tribe of Levi *(page 126)*

**magi** the wise men who came to worship the newborn Jesus in Bethlehem *(page 47)*

**Messiah** 'anointed one', a spiritual leader sent by God to help people on earth return to God's laws *(page 16)*

**monotheistic** believing in one god *(pages 34, 80)*

**moral** concerned with the principles of right and wrong *(page 4)*

**multicultural** made up of people from many different cultures *(page 62)*

**myth** a story which is used to describe an important belief using language that is colourful or relates to the supernatural *(pages 30, 208)*

**opinion** someone's personal view on a subject *(pages 30, 136, 190, 230)*

**oppressed** experiencing hardship or unjust treatment through the actions of others *(page 144)*

**oppression** cruel or unjust treatment *(page 148)*

**ordination** the act of admitting a priest to the ministry *(page 12)*

**Original Sin** the first sin in the world, when Adam and Eve ate from the tree that God had forbidden to them. Christians believe that all humans are born with Original Sin *(page 118)*

**pacifism** using peaceful methods to achieve an aim *(pages 194, 234)*

**pacifist** someone who believes that war is wrong *(page 190)*

**palliative care** working to help ease the pain of someone who is dying *(page 164)*

**penicillin** a medicine that is used to fight infection *(page 200)*

**persecuted** someone being punished because of, for example, their beliefs *(pages 38, 234)*

**pilgrimage** a journey to a special place *(page 50)*

**Pope** the Bishop of Rome who is the leader of the Roman Catholic Church *(pages 4, 50)*

**prejudice** an opinion formed without knowledge or reason *(pages 148, 230)*

**priest** a person with the authority to perform religious ceremonies *(pages 4, 42, 104, 126, 194, 242)*

**private worship** when a person worships on their own *(page 42)*

**promiscuous** having many casual sexual relationships *(page 156)*

**proof** evidence that something is true or exists *(pages 30, 69, 110, 200)*

**prophecy** a prediction of the future, believed to come from God *(page 30)*

**prophet** someone who receives a message or inspiration from God *(page 16)*

**public worship** when groups of people worship together *(page 42)*

**Purgatory** a place of purification *(page 84)*

**Quaker** a member of the Christian denomination otherwise known as the Religious Society of Friends *(pages 42, 153, 190)*

**rape** sex without consent *(page 160)*

**reconciliation** coming together again after disagreement *(page 122)*

**resurrected** raised from the dead *(pages 16, 34, 88)*

**revelation** something revealed that was previously hidden *(pages 58, 92, 204)*

**right** the moral or legal claim to have or do something *(pages 104, 136, 190, 238)*

**sacrament** a religious ceremony which is the outward visible sign of an inward spiritual grace *(pages 118, 156, 242)*

**sacred** considered to be special and holy *(pages 50, 153, 178)*

**sacred writings** texts that are important and special to religious people as they tell them about their faith and which they believe to have been inspired by God *(pages 20, 27)*

**Salvation Army** a Christian organisation actively working within the community *(page 182)*

**Samaritan** a person belonging to a religion closely associated with Judaism *(page 126)*

**sanctity of life** the belief that life is sacred or holy *(page 153)*

**scriptures** holy or sacred writings *(pages 34, 204)*

**secular** having no spiritual or religious basis *(pages 62, 164)*

**soul** the spiritual part of a human regarded as immortal *(pages 69, 160, 224)*

**stereotyping** taking a generalised, oversimplified view of a group of people, which is usually negative *(page 230)*

**stewardship** looking after something for someone else *(pages 92, 140, 174, 224)*

**suicide** killing yourself intentionally *(page 164)*

**supernatural** something thought to be the result of a force beyond scientific understanding or the laws of nature *(page 30)*

**symbol** an action, image, object or picture that is used to represent something else *(pages 38, 76)*

**Ten Commandments** a set of rules given by God to Moses, which Jews and Christians try to follow in their lives *(pages 20, 34)*

**terminally ill** suffering from a fatal disease *(page 164)*

**theist** someone who believes there is a God *(page 72)*

**theory of evolution** the idea that all species living today are the result of a process of development that began with simple life forms more than three billion years ago *(page 208)*

**transcendent** beyond human understanding *(page 80)*

**Trinity** the mystery of one God in three persons: Father, Son and Holy Spirit *(pages 34, 80)*

**virgin** a person who has not had sex *(pages 16, 156)*

**vocation** a feeling that someone is 'called' to follow a certain career, possibly by God *(page 12)*

**worship** to show love, respect or devotion to someone or something *(pages 4, 27, 72, 242)*